Down the U-Bend
of Your Mind

Down the U-Bend of Your Mind

A Look at Self-Examination

KEVIN BARNARD

authorHOUSE®

AuthorHouse™ UK
1663 Liberty Drive
Bloomington, IN 47403 USA
www.authorhouse.co.uk
Phone: 0800.197.4150

Scripture quotations are taken from the Holy Bible, New International Version®. NIV®. Copyright © 1973, 1978, 1984 by International Bible Society. Used by permission of Zondervan. All rights reserved.

Published by AuthorHouse 09/07/2015

ISBN: 978-1-5049-8847-6 (sc)
ISBN: 978-1-5049-8848-3 (e)

Print information available on the last page.

Contents

Preface

This little book is intensely practical, for it is about being human. It began as a parish Lent course.

Traditionally, the following pages would come some way into a much larger book on what is known as moral theology. (Personally, I would like to read a book about immoral theology.) I hope, in time, that there will be a successor to this book dealing with some of the bigger issues raised here, but it seemed good to begin at what might be called the obviously practical level. Although written from a Christian position and drawing on Christian resources, I believe much of what the book contains will be of interest to others and may even help them understand something of Christianity better.

I should say something about the style used in this book. First, there are good reasons for avoiding the first person; after all, constant use of the word I is irritating in ordinary conversation and 'I' can sound too much as though the book is simple autobiography. In a book of this sort, however, I thought I might allow myself to use that pronoun for the sake of ease. (As I did in that sentence!) This book draws on autobiography, and on a wet afternoon an under-employed therapist might try to work out what specific bits are autobiography. I am not sure. I can say that I have extensive acquaintance with various kinds of failure in myself but what is here offered is based in large measure on experiences that have helped me. I work on the assumption that most people are normal, and that I might, therefore, be helping by sharing.

The second point about style is to comment on the use of capital letters. I follow what may now seem an old-fashioned practice of using capital letters when referring to God or the Persons of the Trinity by pronouns or in using possessive adjectives in connexion with Them or when referring to the Life of Jesus. Habits can be helpful.

I should also say a word about the subtitle of this book. If we were in the eighteenth century I might have written something like 'Self-examination examined'. I hope this book will help people in the practice of self-examination, but the very practice needs to be examined. As will be explained, it can cause hurt rather than healing, it can bring temptation, it can enable a wholly inappropriate kind of defence to be erected around the life of the individual. Also, there is a danger that cultivating the practice of self-examination will be seen as distinctive of only one part of the church. No Christian can evade it - 'Judge therefore yourselves that you be not judged by the Lord.' I suspect many readers will look and after a few pages will say that they already do something of this sort, they will feel as though they are on familiar territory after all.

I owe all kinds of debts to all kinds of people. The late Gordon Roe taught a group of us at Durham on the subject of hearing confessions, but he taught me much more than that, and I am grateful. His successor as priest-in-charge at Saint Michael's, Abingdon, the late John Andrew, also helped greatly in my formation, though he was a very different man in many ways and for him also I have cause to give thanks, as also for the whole community of that church. Long may it flourish and bear witness to a form of Christian life not now much honoured, though useful in the life of the whole church.

To those other priests who have heard my confessions over the years I owe a debt that only God can pay. I pray for them, as the form of confession requires, but I also give thanks for them.

To those who have sought in kindly (or less-than-kindly) ways to show me my shortcomings, I owe much of the material in this book.

The quotation at the end of chapter four is from a lecture given by Professor Leo Missine on ageing.

As for the first of the last two sentences in the book, it comes from a well-known source; as for the second, it is something I have been saying to people in various situations for a long time, but only recently have I encountered it in Walter Farrell O.P.'s *Companion to the Summa*. I am sure it did not start with either of us, but for all that it states the obvious it still seems worth saying.

The story in chapter four is fiction. The reader can discover the truth.

This book may be used in a variety of ways, but some readers might find it helpful to read it as a group or to read it under guidance. I must exhort you, if you are in any way troubled by reading this book, to seek the help of a minister of the church. More likely, however, you may think, 'What is all the fuss about?' But this book is offered with and in the hope that it will help some folk as the exercises discussed have helped me. It is not bogus piety or some form of window dressing that makes me say that I pray for any who may read these pages and ask their prayers for me.

Above all, under God, I thank my children, Deborah and Jonathan, for their patience in many ways, and my wife, Catherine, who has shared in so much of my work and given more than priestly support, though we differ fundamentally on whether one travels in a bus or a 'bus.

Introduction

Loving God, one's neighbour – and oneself?

When Jesus was asked to name the chief commandment, He gave as the first that we should love God wholeheartedly. And then he said that we should love our neighbours as ourselves. It is easy to rush over the *as ourselves* bit. Does it not go without saying that we love ourselves?

The answer to that is a definite 'No' – and in more ways than one.

To love something or somebody is to value and care for her/him/it. Much that we do or might do is harmful to ourselves, whether physically or morally, socially or spiritually or psychologically, if it is possible to separate those different areas. Doctors regularly advise against smoking, but what we see or hear and how we see or hear can affect the way we relate to others. We can damage ourselves that way.

Again, we can take on all the negative things about ourselves, real or imaginary, and come to hate ourselves. To be self-satisfied is dangerous, but to be eaten up with self-loathing or views of oneself that are wholly negative is just as damaging. There is much that contributes to the formation of negative self-images. Think of advertising, which works by generating dissatisfaction, by making the observers think they are lesser beings if they lack what the advertiser is selling.

To love oneself is not the same as being selfish or self-satisfied. It is simply to know that one is valued - and that means valued by another. To value oneself and see that as enough is to go down the path to selfishness or self-satisfaction. To know one is valued both reassures and humbles, without humiliation.

The subject of this book, self-examination, can seem like an exercise in negativity. It certainly is not, but it demands a certain stance of readiness to be humble and honest. Often, we can be our own worst critics or judges. That is why it is often helpful to do this kind of exercise in the setting of a dialogue, and that is part of the value of formal confession. But a dialogue can also be provided by less formal conversation. Further, if one practises self-examination on one's own there is still a dialogue partner: a part of oneself (which has its own dangers) or God. To put oneself consciously and deliberately in the presence of God is to invite a conversation partner. It also can lead to a review of one's idea of God. Look at the results of the self-examination and see how far the god who would lead you to such conclusions conforms to the image of God as revealed in Scripture. If there is a discrepancy then, perhaps your idea of God needs to be revised.

This can then lead to a better love of God, that is, to a better fulfilling of the first commandment, for if we love someone or something we want to know them better and as we get to know them better so the more we can love them. Jesus calls people to look beyond themselves and to look toward the unlimited and ultimately undefineable. We are not to be curved in on self. 'Humanity curved in on self' is one traditional way of speaking of the condition of sin.

And once we are not curved in on self, then we are led to look around as well as up, to look at how we relate, as valued parts, to a greater context, human and non-human, each part of which is also valued and commended to our love, and to understand how we should live. This, unfortunately, is not a single event. In the following pages we shall look at some of the ways in which we can come to curve in on self.

The dangers of apologizing

We have probably all been in situations where we have apologized and then wondered why we did so. Or perhaps you know (or are) the kind of person who apologizes as a defence mechanism, apologizing for one thing when the real fault is something else. This is not just a neurotic exercise. We manipulate for reassurance or we seek to hide the fault of which we are only partly aware.

Again, there is a danger in apologizing to which Christians are especially liable. We apologize to God routinely. Many church services include a prayer of confession. First, this can make us feel, once we have confessed and been absolved, that there is no more to be done. By spending their time apologizing to God, many Christians seem to think they are released from any need to apologize to anyone else!

Further, there is the problem that the prayers of confession, because they are formalized, lose their full meaning. *Yes, we know we have to do that bit, now we have got it out the way let's get on …* If we use any prayer of confession, we need to ask ourselves what it is for which we are saying sorry; otherwise, we are no different from those people who compulsively go to police stations and own up to crimes they have not committed. This approach does not serve any purpose and can, in fact, be harmful, for it can formalize sin and dull us to the sense of its seriousness. It can also prevent the healing work of God in leading us from sin through grace to life, but to say that is to run ahead of much of this book.

Self-examination should free us from these dangers. To know why and to Whom or whom we are apologizing, to know whether we need to apologize and to know how we are to alter our behaviour are key issues in growth as human beings and as Christians.

What this book is not

It is hoped that non-Christians will find this book helpful for any reasonable person must at some time ask herself/himself questions of the sort raised here. But this is not a handbook of moral theology, indicating what counts as sin and how serious each sin might be. It is, perhaps, a way to giving a context in which each person can raise such questions.

This book is not an alternative to any form of counselling or therapy or medication. These all have their place in the scheme of things, and many people are helped by them. Christians should rejoice that they are available and remember that Jesus spent a lot of time healing. In fact, the gospels say more about that side of His ministry than about His words of condemnation.

In the light of that, a distinction needs to be made. What is a normal human being? This book is written for normal human beings (by definition, most of us). Yet, in all our lives, there have been things that have harmed, knocked and chipped us. Our responses and behaviours can be the result of influences which are wrong, influences internalized in our early days that now work without our being aware of them. Amateur psychoanalysis is dangerous, but sometimes a realistic look at one's life journey, a look at those influences which have shaped one, can be part of the healing process. To grow up in an unloving atmosphere makes it hard to love. Yet a process of self-examination which begins with an affirmation of one's value can lead to repair work over the course of time. Whatever the cause, a sin remains a sin, something which has no place in the world as God intends it. But that does not mean that the degree of culpability is always the same. This book is not about psychoanalysis; rather, it is about affirming the value of all people and looking at how we might individually live better lives in the light of the knowledge that we, all of us, are loved and are capable of loving.

1. "Know Yourself"

To begin at the beginning ...

Once upon a time ... there was a golden age of a church which cultivated sanctity with the aid of rigorous self-examination and spectacular penitential practices.

From the earliest times in the church, the practice of self-examination has been observed. Paul exhorts his readers to examine themselves, and that exhortation is taken up in the Church of England's *Book of Common Prayer*, in which we are told: 'Judge, therefore, yourselves..that ye be not judged of the Lord.'[1]

In the Roman Catholic Church it was the norm until recently to receive communion only after going to confession, whilst in the Orthodox Church there is the account (in the spiritual classic *The Way of a Pilgrim*) of how, though the pilgrim has regularly attended services, he has to go to confession when he wants to receive communion.

In the Church of Scotland, the approach of Sacrament Sunday entails a time of examination and penitence. By this process one can seek grace to amend one's life and be aware of one's share in causing the Death commemorated in the sacrament and be led to deeper devotion to Jesus.

In Methodism, class leaders had the task of asking of those committed to their charge how they had grown in the faith.

Both Catholic and Evangelical Anglicans have practised self-examination, especially before receiving communion. Frequently, this has been done with the aid of manuals of devotion or books of prayers, often given to candidates preparing for confirmation.

Yet the practice seems to have been neglected of late. Some people have argued that it has created problems, inducing anxiety or a sense of failure. It is hard to prove such a point, for no one can say whether a particular person would have suffered had they not practised their particular form of self-examination. On the other hand, those who promote the practice by pointing to the glories of the past cannot claim those achievements as proof of its value. Were people disciplined and vigorous in the practice of their faith because they practised self-examination or did they practise self-examination because they were disciplined? Even, did they accept discipline because there was no alternative? Also, we have no way of telling the amount of individual growth or the amount of agony endured by unknown millions of ordinary believers. (Certainly, at least one person is known to have been twice driven to the brink of suicide by the Commination, the service in the Church of England's *Book of Common Prayer* which marks the start of Lent. The particular case in mind is, of course, confidential, but if the service is read it will be seen how, for someone already in a particular state of mind, it could cause anxiety. In most editions of the *Book of Common Prayer* this service will be found immediately before the Psalms.)

All this, however, is not to begin at the beginning! Self-examination for the Christian is not the same as some form of self-analysis. Indeed, there is a danger of misplaced emphasis that can turn the practice into a source of self-congratulation. No one doubts that the Pharisee in the parable of the Pharisee and the tax-collector (Luke 18.9 - 14) practised self-examination! Or the misplaced emphasis can lead to unrelieved self-loathing. This may be because we think of the label as meaning examination *by* oneself. If one is left alone with such a task it is not surprising that problems may occur. Such a case is like that of the person who reads a medical encyclopaedia and believes s/he needs no other help or believes s/he is afflicted with every imaginable illness - and some unimaginable ones!

What should happen is examination *of* oneself, an honest and thorough exposition of one's symptoms in the presence of God. For it is God Who is examining, and the whole process would be better received and more sanely practised if we (the church) were readier to use medical rather than judicial comparisons. In the gospels we read of Jesus denouncing sinful behaviour and corrupt values, but we also read of Him healing. This latter aspect of His ministry has been set aside or treated in a fundamentalistic way. Jesus the moral teacher has been turned into Jesus the judge, and one image we need to remember has predominated. Might not many anxious people be helped if they could be encouraged to talk to Jesus as to a wise family physician who knows all about his patients and their circumstances? Of course, diagnosis can sometimes bring pain, and treatment can be arduous. But we can speak of treatment, which is for the good of the recipient, as well as punishment, which is for whose good? If it is for the recipient's good, then we are back to curing. And can it be of any eternal value to those who have suffered at the hands of a wrongdoer? Surely some of the nastiest Christian literature must be that found among some of the writings of such as Tertullian or Bernard of Cluny, who both spoke of the consolation those who have suffered for the faith will find in the eventual punishment of the evil.

Such writers gave systematic expression to an attitude that probably lurks beneath the surface in many of us. If God condemns, He does it for reasons we may or may not be told, but which it is no business of ours to pry into as voyeurs or to try to fathom for ourselves as though we were demi-gods who could anticipate how God will dole out justice.

Another image that might be useful – though it is not explicitly biblical – is that of God as the theatrical producer. We have our parts to play even though there is no rehearsal for life. But as each scene passes, the producer can ask us, "What was going on in that scene? Are you being a consistent character? And how will your character evolve if you carry on in that way? What was going on in your head and heart in that scene? And what was revealed to the audience of One?" Actors, notoriously, live on the edge of their nerves. Is *oneself* the hardest part to play?

And this helps to take us back to a beginning. Once upon a time … there was a child who wondered at the world, enjoyed it, and feared it, and learned to survive in it. Over the course of time, that child became aware of being part of the world and from being done to began to do. And that child is you and I - and the human race. Throughout our lives there is in all of us a *child-part*, a *partner-part* and a *parent-part*. Living is about the harmonious flourishing of these parts, sometimes separately, sometimes together.

The issue here is a tension between *integrity* and *integration*. We all want to survive, and that means retaining our integrity. But we also want – and need – to belong, and that means integration. Someone may preserve integrity at the cost of isolation or the loss of any standard of reference by which to guide their behaviour. Someone may achieve too great a degree of integration, securely wrapped up in that to which they belong and unable to criticize it or survive its demise. This tension exists in the church, the family, and the state. In the twentieth century, Nazi Germany gave an example of both, with a leader who seemed to retain integrity and sought to dominate by demanding great integration. In a family, a domineering parent can seek to survive without changing by threatening the integrity of every other member of the family.

Another balance that needs to be maintained, then, is that between the outward-regarding and the inward-looking parts of our life. *What will my integration do to myself and others? Is a given course of action going to threaten the integrity by which I identify myself – as, for example, a religious conversion may do?*

Traditionally, the balance between emotions and intellect has been seen as important. Often in Christian settings emotions have been channelled – into art or music or into dedication to good works, for instance, – and the intellect has been seen as necessarily "in control". (Such a view is in itself dangerous. Without emotion would there be art or music, and would good works merely become desiccated formalities? This is, of course, too big an issue to be dealt with in parentheses, but it is an issue nonetheless.) Yet Christians do not need to fear the point made by a (non-Christian) philosopher, that "reason is... the slave of the passions".[2] Our commitments often precede our reasons for making them, and emotion can use reason to judge emotions. Part of the price of human freedom, paradoxically, is that there is for human beings on their own no such thing as *the reasonable thing to do*. There is only what it is reasonable to do (or think) *if* one seeks certain ends or espouses certain values.

What is being presented is a view of human life as not a well worked-out system but a continuous balancing act.

Perhaps we can see it as comparable to the sailing of a boat when the only means of propulsion were sails and oars. We may adjust the sail, but there will be times when we do not keep to our course as well as we might. Moral and spiritual development are about learning to steer – and when to put one's oar in!

And that takes us to another *once upon a time*. Once upon a time, there were a man and a woman in a garden. You know the story. The wrong turning taken brought disaster, but the turning was a turning away from love, and the disaster was to be remedied by love.

That is the message of the Bible. And that is what makes self-examination bearable, for it is a means of sensing the wind and learning to respond to it, to continue the comparison with sailing, it is, or should be, a reminder for particular circumstances of knowing that we start from God and are meant for life with Him. Our self-examination is to be more like checking the map as we travel than anxiously wondering whether we are beautiful statues for God's collection. God made us, and He made us for the journey. If things go wrong, we do not succeed in our journeying if we quarrel with one another or grow angry with ourselves - and we know turning back was never an option. All we can do, all we need to learn to do is value the goal of the journey and know that we are not travelling alone.

But what about ...?

Something has already been said of the dangers of self-examination, and we need to be aware of them.

The first – and one that is easier to fall into than many – is that of making it a virtue in its own right. Somehow, an awareness of one's sins can be made into a reason for deeming oneself superior. One possible reason for this is the fact that to many people self-examination sounds like a very elevated thing, a deeply *spiritual thing* (whatever that might mean). And there is enough of the worldling in us to use that estimate to flatter ourselves. *If other people don't do this, are afraid to do it, then I must be special for doing it.* Self-examination is not an end in its own right, not a game to be played for itself. If you are a sinner (and self-examination, whatever else it does, will show that you are), you are not improved by becoming a narcissistic sinner. It is not the fault of self-examination if someone ends up wallowing in or adding to their sins.

Secondly, there is what might be called the Lot's wife syndrome. Lot's wife was turned into a pillar of salt when she looked back on the cities of the plain as they were destroyed. Self-examination can re-awaken sinfulness. As I remember my reaction to Smith (the time-honoured name for all anonymous figures), my anger, say, I slip, at first imperceptibly, into looking at why I was angry. (*Surely this is an important thing to do?*) And then I begin to look for excuses, and then I blame the situation on Smith. I thus come to the point of denying my sin and add to it by re-writing the past and nursing a fresh anger against Smith. Here, it would seem, a too-careful scrutiny produces the problem. The danger might seem to lie in the attempted self-analysis rather than in the examination. Looking for a reason in this way is like the activity of a board of enquiry, inviting submissions on behalf of the accused – myself –and engaging my fondness for myself, including my attachment to my anger. And, from of old, writers have been aware of how someone's confrontation with their sexual sins or temptations can excite further temptation.

To say that there is no easy answer seems like avoiding an answer. However, this liability to further temptation and sin can serve as an indicator of the nature of the problem. We are not caught on a treadmill of being unable to look inside ourselves for fear of increasing what makes the looking painful. To use a medical analogy again, it can be said that the pain of extracting a tooth and the pain of tooth-ache can come very close – and the former is a consequence of the latter. In the same way, the system automatically reacts when the sore point of temptation is touched. This occurrence underlines the fact that in self-examination we are handing over our whole selves to God, we are describing the symptoms to the doctor, and if further problems come to light then that is all the more reason for consulting the doctor, not a reason for avoiding him.

It might be thought that monks of the Eastern Church would be particularly rigorous and expect us to flay ourselves, especially a monk named Mark the Ascetic. However, some words of that monk, who wrote in the fifth century, are very much to the point. He writes:

> To recall past sins in detail inflicts injury on the man who hopes in God. For when such recollection brings remorse it deprives him of hope; but if he pictures the sins to himself without remorse, they pollute him again with the old defilement.[3]

There is the danger of picking at a scab! As children probably many of us were told not to do that, however fascinating it might be, because the healing process can be delayed. Nevertheless, if we look at those words again they do leave open some space for recollection. When I am not aware of something as a sin, I do not have to recall it. There is sufficient detail in what I lay before God. Yet, as I continue in the life of faith, greater depths of sin, or sinfulness, may be revealed, and then I should renew my penitence. In seeking a sense of proportion in this process, Saint Francis deSales (1567–1622) can help. Certainly, he took sin and the need for repentance seriously, but he could also offer counsel such as the following:

> As we consider our sins in detail, let us consider God's graces in detail. ... If sin abounds in malice to ruin us, grace superabounds to restore us ... Christ was more concerned with St. Peter's repentance and remorse than with his sin ...
>
> Lift up your heart quite tranquilly when it falls, humbling yourself before God by acknowledging your misery, without being in the least astonished at your fall .... Well! my poor heart, here we are, fallen into the ditch which we had made so firm a resolution to avoid; ah! let us rise and leave it forever.
>
> Courage! henceforth let us be more on our guard, God will help us, we shall do well enough![4]

There is help here. Saint Francis encourages us to look to God, not to be obsessed with our failings. Above all, perhaps, we should learn to live out the meaning of Saint Paul's words that we have died to sin. If we can see sin as something dead, it need no longer frighten us.

In this as in much else, simplicity is essential. And simplicity can deliver us from the "board of enquiry" view of self-examination. It was said earlier that there is a difference between self-examination and self-analysis. Though much despised, the old-fashioned lists of sins found in certain books of devotion have a place. God knows, better than we do, any extenuating circumstances. All we have to do is lay before Him what is on our hearts. Perhaps here a point about religious language needs to be borne in mind. The basic form of religious speech is the command, not the proposition. Whether we are interested in or fully understand what God says to us does not matter. What matters is how we respond.

Self-analysis begins by looking at what there is inside oneself and trying to make connexions between that and one's experiences and actions. But a different way of viewing the process of growth is to say that what is inside is formed by and from what is outside. There is a great fear of *heteronomy* – that is, being governed by external rules to which one has given no authentic consent. While this may be useful as a precaution in dealing with any human institution, there is a need to remember that, whether we like it or not, the universe just is this way. Indeed, the quest for autonomy before God is the theme of the story of Adam and Eve.

Even without resorting to religious language, we can see how people – we – are influenced by what is on the outside. Since before we were aware or capable of realizing what was happening, we have been receiving instructions, commands. These commands have taken many forms. There have been the straightforward directives given in childhood as to how we should behave, but there have also been the implicit commands, absorbed from our family and home. Some form of the following phrases may sound familiar: "This is the way to survive here; this is the way to flourish, win approval or get what you want."

And this process continues. Instructions or directives are given within workplaces, not only in obvious ways (such as being told how to do the job), but in subtle ways (such as letting one know how to do the job with a particular group of people). Through the media, we are being *persuaded*, that is, gently told, how to think, which life-style we should value, and how we should spend our time and money. Popular morality – and the moral views of many who consider themselves above the popular level – is formed not so much by conscious decisions as to what is right or wrong as by awareness of what is possible. Such awareness influences people's decisions about spending on the latest "must-have" boys' toy, as popular gadgets are now called, whether a mobile 'phone or a four-wheel drive car. It can even influence decisions about the pursuit of scientific research, as the knowledge that something can be done easily leads to the decision that it should be done. (This is an extension of the story of Adam and Eve, in which the fruit was seen to be attractive.)

We are already involved in doing things. Self-examination is not an optional extra; rather, it is a way of discerning which instructions we are following, what is behind them (if anything) and how we are to go about fulfilling them, if we should. It is at this point that self-analysis is of use, the search for those hidden instructions which may be dictating behaviour more in line with survival than growth. The question one must ask oneself is as follows: *What do I do with the results of all this?*

Here the danger of depression or despair rears its head – the remorse that deprives us of hope (as mentioned by Mark the Ascetic). If we are left to ourselves in this, it will be a depressing process. After all, by ourselves, we are left with all the dirty linen spilling out of the bag and no way to deal with it. If we try to be honest, we are afraid of 'letting myself off the hook'. If instructions are called into question and we are led to see harm done to ourselves or others as the result of following certain ways, we are still left wondering what to follow and worrying about how to remedy the past. If that were all there needed to be said, it would be far better to keep the lid on everything and go through life like those whose confidence is overbearing. Such people never apologize because they dare not face the fact of having made a mistake. The world and the church are littered with such people, and most of us have resorted to schemes which, on reflection, will be seen to be like that at one time or another.

We are created by and for God, and God does not make mistakes and does not give up. (How's that for a working summary of the Bible!) Our gaze should rest on God, not on ourselves. At the time of the Reformation, Martin Luther, who had suffered from a sense of his own sinfulness and finally won through to freedom by grasping the message of Paul's Letter to the Romans, spoke of the state of despair as being the situation when someone was curved in on himself/herself, *incurvatus in se*, leaving himself or herself to - just himself or herself.

Self-examination without God is purely destructive. It can lead to depression or to pride or to paralysis. Even the few inches of self-improvement that can be achieved can be dangerous. One of the principles of Alcoholics Anonymous, which is deliberately *not* a religious group in the sense of promoting adherence to a particular faith, is the opening up of each member to her/his higher power, however conceived. One can learn from one's mistakes, certainly, but where is the goal toward which that learning is directed? And who defines a mistake?

"God, I thank You ..."

Those words of the Pharisee in the parable (Luke 18:9–14) lead on in his case to boasting. However, they are not a bad way to begin self-examination. In the psalms the speaker often beats himself up, but there are also times of thanksgiving for the good experienced by the community and the individual.

The English suffer from misplaced good manners. We are taught not to boast (which, of course, we should not do). But this protects our sense that our achievements really are our own. "I don't talk about that because it might seem that I am showing off," can really mean "I don't want to flaunt my superiority." If the speaker began by asking what would constitute showing off it might enable her/him to speak more straightforwardly. As a first, positive step in self-examination, it might be helpful to look for the times when we have got something right. We can then learn to give thanks for it because it is the gift of God's grace. Thinking about a situation carefully – *How did I keep my cool in that situation? I don't know. Thank You, God.* – might help us learn to accept our dependence upon God. Or we might acknowledge that God has listened by musing, *Where did I find those words to say to that person? I don't know. Thank You, God.* This might well be appropriate as a follow-on if we have said the prayer of Saint Francis 'Lord, make me an instrument of Your peace', and the situation has been one in which peace was achieved. And even if we do know where the words came from, we can still give thanks that they were supplied. We can grow in gratitude for the good in our past, the things that have fed us and equipped us. We see this form of gratitude in the psalms.

God doesn't give prizes; He gives life. The mistake of the Pharisee was to think in terms of comparison. If you have ever felt the temptation to be greedy or adulterous, then you have grounds for gratitude when you have resisted the temptation. There is also reason to be grateful if one has been spared temptation. So, another kind of gratitude, one that might support the virtue of resignation, is gratitude for being spared from certain situations. One might fruitfully think, *Being the kind of person I am, God, I thank You that I am not … a manager (or a teacher, or a judge, or a bishop or married to … or living in … or single &c.).* The Pharisee would have learned a lot if he had said, "God, I thank You that I have not been tempted in the same way as this man beside me has been tempted …" (There is a danger here of curiosity. The Pharisee would have no business asking how the tax-collector has been tempted, but he knows he will have been. He does not know, however, how, or even whether, the tax-collector has sinned. All he can say is that he, the Pharisee, has not had to face the temptations he knows will come with the tax-collector's job. When some problem is well known, detailed knowledge is not essential.)

So, where to begin?

Despite what was said about the difference between self-examination and self-analysis, if we believe in God as a loving creator, it makes sense to see His will for us as not an arbitrary set of commands that we are to obey for His sake, but rather as guidance we are to follow for our sake. We make a break between rules for eating rightly, what is meant by healthy eating, or exercising rightly and rules for ordering our lives rightly. Why?

Again, it was suggested earlier that the examination, though it is of the self, is not to be done simply by oneself alone. With that in mind, we can find aids for self-examination more readily by turning to aids which are available in the Bible. So, just to get going, here are one or two possible tools for self-examination.

First, read Psalm 23. This has little to do with the detailed process of self-examination but a lot to do with how we should start and end it. Remember what was said about the parts of our selves. We are bringing the child part as to a parent who agonizes for us and wants us to grow. We are bringing the partner part to acknowledge our infidelity (we could draw on the Book of Hosea to think of this). We are bringing the parent part to One Who has trusted us, that is, God, made Himself vulnerable to draw out our love, and Whom we have let down. How will He respond? In this psalm come the words of confidence that give a setting for what we are about to do.

Secondly, there are the Ten Commandments (Exodus 20:1–17). In these there is as much psychology as ethics. *How many gods are there in my life? What forms of idolatry do I practise, to restrict God or manipulate the world? How seriously do I take God's identification of Himself with me?* These are the kinds of questions prompted by a more than superficial reading of the Commandments. It is impossible for any one person to write an exhaustive list, for the questions will reflect what is on the mind of the honest reader at the time. I may not have stolen from a shop, yet who but God and I can easily identify the forms my thieving has taken recently?

Thirdly, there is Our Lord's Summary of the Law (Mark 12:29–31). It is tempting to see this as introducing love, as if such a notion were absent from the Ten Commandments. However, this summary is no easy alternative. To love God with all one's strength is to love Him with all that gives one any kind of power. So do I choose for Him in my life as a citizen (seeking the kingdom of God in politics), or with my money (by which I exercise power over millions in this country and overseas), or with my talents (by which I can, perhaps, perform some service which seems negligible to me but which makes a great difference in the life of someone else)? For me to love with all my mind means seeking to be conformed in my thinking to the way of God – so do I escape into a private fantasy realm where I am still in control?

Fourthly, there is the list of the fruit of the Spirit (Galatians 5:22–23). It is important to remember that this is a list of things coming from the Spirit, not a list of virtues to be pursued and practised. If I notice in my life a lack of these things, I am not to try harder to be joyful or gentle, for example, just by expending a bit more energy or just by making a resolution 'I *will* be joyful'. Such a resolution will not last and could make me a pain to others while I am trying to keep it. Instead, I should seek afresh the Spirit that was given to me at baptism. Yes, the gift is already there, but I need to ask honestly and humbly for its work. God was always with the Israelites in the wilderness, but they had to learn that He was there, and what that meant. Just so in our lives, the fact that we may not now be feeling very patient does not mean that the Spirit Who supplies patience is not there. We are being led back to a new recognition of dependence.

Fifthly, there are Our Lord's words at the institution of the Eucharist. The Self-giving love of God is supremely displayed in the Life and Death of Jesus. Think: *Do I treasure and respond to that love? Jesus spoke of a new covenant. Do I live as a member of the covenant community? The blood is shed for many. Do I see others as so valued in and by Jesus that He thought they were worth dying for? Do I seek to help others enter into the covenant relationship?*

Sixthly, there are the Beatitudes (Matthew 5:3–11). These can be read in various ways, but they reverse many popular judgements – in the first century *and* in the twenty-first century. They are not points on a check-list to be ticked off. They invite the giving of time to reflection and prayer and action. Here, we may find a portrait of Jesus underlying the portrait of true humanity.

Seventhly, there is the description of love in 1 Corinthians 13. Think: *As well as the obvious (!) points listed, do I recognize my incompleteness? Do I look to the future as simply a matter of more of the same, with limited variations, or do I look forward to the new in Christ?* In this chapter, too, there is a portrait of Jesus.

But then again ...

With so much material, it might seem perverse to go outside the Bible. However, three other ways of setting about self-examination deserve to be mentioned.

First, there are relationships. We need different relationships, so we can need to check how healthy these are. Think: *What is my relationship with God like? Am I honest with Him? Do I let Him be honest with me? What is my relationship with the church like? or with my family? or with my friends? or with those with whom I work? or with the (human) world? or with the rest of creation? or with myself?* Questions about gratitude and selfishness may emerge, but my love of my neighbour (or my lack of it) may reflect my relationship with myself.

Secondly, there are the so-called seven deadly sins. This is where we get technical for a minute. From very early days, writers have tried to define, list and classify sins. In the Middle Ages it was reckoned that every sin could be placed under one of seven headings. These seven headings were called the *septem peccata capitalia,* the seven capital (heading) sins. Unfortunately, the word *capital* had more than one meaning. It could refer to a heading (this is where it is related to our English word *chapter*), or it could refer to a crime for which one lost one's head (just as in England, certain offences were known as *capital offences,* and the death penalty was referred to as *capital punishment*). When the Latin came to be translated, it was taken in the second sense, as if those sins were deadly. But what other sins are there?

The list seems fairly comprehensive: pride, lechery, envy, anger, avarice, gluttony, and sloth.

It can be a harrowing experience to look for these in their different forms in one's life.

Thirdly, there are the questions of seeking and evading. In all our actions we are either seeking or evading something – even if we are only scratching an itch! To ask, *What am I seeking in this action or speech or thought?* or (or sometimes "and") *What am I evading?* can reveal important things about oneself. Of course, one has to be honest. After all, the only one listening besides God is oneself. You cannot deceive the former and there is no point in deceiving the latter.

On behalf of rules

In recent times, rules have been distrusted. To act in accordance with one's conscience has been thought more important. Conscience is important, but this supposed conflict is a false polarization. How is one's conscience formed? A significant part of that process of formation stems from the rules instilled in us by the institutions and relationships amidst which we grew up. And if I am to give expression to the judgement of my conscience, there will be implicit in that statement (if not explicit) some rule or other.

There can be a smugness or complacency that comes from 'obeying the rules' and the idea can arise that, so long as one obeys the rules, the rest of one's life is entirely at one's personal disposal. There is a proper resistance to the idea or the possibility that we may become robots. But we are not called to robotic obedience. The rules exist to protect us and to enable us to grow. We can reasonably ask why there is a particular rule. This might lead to the rejection of the rule, but it can also lead to the development of the rule and a growth in understanding of oneself. In a given situation, we may say, 'This rule works because human beings are liable to do ...' From that we can go on to ask, 'How then do we counter that liability and achieve healing for the individual and the community?'

What next?

A few questions for reflection:
Why have we become shy of talking about individual sin?

When was the last time you apologized to someone?
How deeply did you mean what you said?
Whose opinion matters to you? How do you set about influencing it?

What in your private life (in thought, word or deed) would you most hate others to discover? Why?

What would you most like other people to know about you?

What would you describe as one of your talents? Why not thank God for it?
What do you look forward to?

Think of a good deed you have done. Give thanks to God for the grace and resources which enabled you to do it.

Some work on the Bible

Read Luke 14:1–6.
What are the things about which you would consider yourself "conservative"? Why?
What are the things about which you would consider yourself "radical"? Why?
What would make you go out on a limb for someone?

Read Luke 15:8–10.
God has given you things to treasure.
What among those things do you think you have lost?
Ask for God's help in recovering it (or them).

Read Luke 18:9–14.
Make out the case in defence of the Pharisee.
How would you sum up the Pharisee's problem?

And finally …

As was said, self-examination has been practised for a long time. However, you may not find what I have stated thus far a congenial way into the practice. So here are a few books by weightier writers. If you did not read this book but did read one of the books listed, you would have gained. If this chapter drives you thus far, this labour will not have been in vain.

In chronological order:
Thomas àKempis *The Imitation of Christ*
William Law *A Serious Call to a Devout and Holy Life*
Soren Kierkegaard *Purity of Heart is to Will One Thing*
William Purcell *The Plain Man Looks at Himself*
D.R. Davies *Down, Peacock's Feathers*
(The first two, though the oldest, are the most easily obtained.)

2. Attack

Cramp in Wonderland

Just at this moment Alice felt a very curious sensation, which puzzled her a good deal until she made out what it was: she was beginning to grow larger again, and she thought at first she would get up and leave the court; but on second thoughts she decided to remain where she was as long as there was room for her.

'I wish you wouldn't squeeze so,' said the Dormouse, who was sitting next to her. 'I can hardly breathe.'

'I can't help it,' said Alice very meekly:'I'm growing.'

'You've no right to grow *here*,' said the Dormouse.

'Don't talk nonsense,' said Alice more boldly:'you know you're growing too.'

'Yes, but *I* grow at a reasonable pace,' said the Dormouse: 'not in that ridiculous fashion.' And he got up very sulkily and crossed over to the other side of the court.

It is possible to do a lot of psychoanalytical work on *Alice in Wonderland*, but the reason for quoting that passage has nothing to do with trying to unravel what was going on in Lewis Carroll's mind (or Freud's), but simply to introduce the topic of growing.

Carroll was writing about a child, and one of the things everybody comments on when looking at children is their growth. "Hasn't he grown since you visited last!" "She'll soon be as tall as Gran.!" Comments like this may embarrass a child, but they are the safe resort for adults who see nothing else remarkable or estimable in the lump of gawky adolescence standing in front of them and who want to communicate welcome, at least to the adults who come with their offspring.

Yet there are all kinds of growth. Indeed, spiritual, intellectual, social and moral exploration are going on all the time. Growth is important; it is a sign of health and life. Yet, as with Alice in the courtroom, space is limited and growth can lead to problems.

Expansion or expansionism?

A word often used in the media to describe policies of which a writer disapproves is *expansionism*. (It is probably just another word for imperialism.) A country exhibits expansionism when it tries to influence another country unfairly or in a way detrimental to that other country or when it is using that country to pursue its own foreign policy.

Expansion might be seen in the growth of a country to realize its potential in industry, for example. Expansionism, though, is a very different matter.

The same distinction can be drawn in looking at individuals. We all have our concerns and interests, the tasks we must fulfil and the duties we must discharge. We seek to grow, whether in developing a hobby or furthering a career or deepening a relationship. And sometimes we see our growth as inextricably tied into the growth of another person or organization, whether the organization or group be big or small, whether it be family, nation, church or bowls club.

The person whose growth is allowed to continue without reference to the growth of others can easily become a pain to those around. The self must grow, but only in the context of relationships. Somebody who pays no regard to others is condemned as, at least, ill-mannered, seen as insensitive and, though s/he may 'get the job done', such a person is likely to have a range of acquaintances and no friends. If such behaviour is carried to extremes it is likely that the person will be diagnosed as suffering from some form of mental or psychiatric problem. And the relationships which matter are not only with other people but with the self and with God. It might seem odd when so many people live as though they deny the existence of God to put that relationship in the list, but if we believe God created the moral order and all true beauty, even those who would deny God are confronted with His works and the outreach of the Spirit. (This is part of the message of the parable of the sheep and goats at Matthew 25:31–46.)

And what does it mean to be in a relationship with oneself? Not only does this mean how we view ourselves, it also entails how the different parts of which we are composed are related to one another. There is an assumption that certain parts of ourselves are to be subordinated to other parts – and perhaps in the case of Christians this has been most obviously the case in the treatment of sexual drives. Somehow, almost anything is meant to claim superiority over sex, which has been viewed as intrinsically 'dirty'. The fact that God wants there to be human beings seems to have been neglected! The Church of England's 1928 Wedding Service, with its talk of the 'natural instincts and affections implanted by God' was surely accurate. To affirm the sexual drive as part of nature is to honour it (as part of God's ordering of the universe) and to put it in its proper place, in relation to the other parts and therefore needing to be kept in harmony with those other parts. Because we live in a sex-obsessed age now, there is the danger in Christian attitudes of imbalance. One danger is that sex is seen as the symbol of and key to all sin. The other danger issues in the pride which claims to rise above something which is actually a divine gift. The same problems can arise, however, with respect to unresolved anger or the urge to accumulate more and more material goods. People are encouraged to "respect their anger," but little is said about what they should then do with it – or how they are to respond when someone else respects her/his own anger in preference to theirs.

Might is right

Yet lurking at the bottom of all this is the question: Why should growth be in any way inhibited? Many who would shrink from an outright assertion that might is right still behave in ways which seem to endorse that view. We do not need to think of politicians; we have probably all met the people who, because they could shout the loudest, have dominated. At least some of us will recognize the times when, through cleverness or an awareness of the way "the system" works, we have been able to get our way, to avoid embarrassment or to win a self-flattering victory. And the quietly spoken, manipulatively self-effacing "saint" could give lessons in control to the Gestapo!

Growth – and that means inevitably the exercise of various powers – is part of God's plan for us. Who sets the limits to the exercise of those powers? And how are the limits justified?

Bluntly, it has to be recognized that, without appealing to any authority outside the world, all systems of law are ways of implementing the policy that might is right, even if the might is being exercised on behalf of the majority of individually weak citizens. And even when appeal is made to a supernatural authority, it is possible to caricature this as an appeal to another form of might. But this is a caricature. If we accept that we are created, then (unless we believe that we are created by some kind of sadistic demon) it is reasonable to think that our well-being is defined by the Creator and achieved by responding obediently, though not resentfully, to Him. From this comes also a justification for government, a justification which sees government as exercising might, but might informed by insights into human nature which are themselves reflections of truths of more than passing convenience.

So?

In growing, we are learning to use the powers given to us. We have to learn to assert ourselves and express ourselves appropriately. But rewards are easily offered for many actions, and when the reward becomes more important than the quality of the action, trouble arises.

Rewards can take the form of a sense of self-satisfaction or they can be material; they can be found in feelings of superiority or in indulgence. And here a seemingly small difference in description makes all the difference in the way we view ourselves. For rewards have to do with doing better than others. One can make the easy step from the belief that one is *infinitely* valued (part of the Christian good news for everybody) to the view that one is *supremely* valuable. The rewards that come in early life, innocent and often necessary, become the goal by which some measure their worth. The elder son in the parable (Luke 15:11-32) might ask: "How many kids has my father given me? And how many am I worth?"

On the attack

Traditionally, pride has been seen as the leading sin, and this is hardly surprising. Pride is about valuing wrongly – having a wrong estimate of oneself and others, but also a wrong view of the place of God and things in one's life. Yet the change of view just mentioned – the attitude which states, "I am supremely important" – leads to wars of aggression.

Because of pride, other people become *things* to serve my will, and things become tools for me to use and discard. Pride drives out gratitude because, after all, if *I* am supremely important, is it not only right that these things should be there to serve me? It is their place in the scheme of things, no less and no more. And as the little empire grows, it is more and more supported by minor triumphs, times when that person, that proud *I*, was proved right. In Britain we are used to the announcement of the Queen's Honours List, when those who have made a significant contribution to the life of the country or the world receive various awards. I can reward myself in an honours list in which I am the sole judge, bestower and recipient. (God, I thank You that I am not like all other men ("Says who, stupid?").) In all this, the use of the first person can be seen as a way of defending the reader and the writer. No one reading this need take offence, because I am not accusing anyone, only myself. But by seeming to write about myself as a formal character, not, of course, the real I, I can divert attention from the times I have really behaved in this way. There is a danger when the game becomes the reality.

And consider what a person becomes when s/he is being self-assertive or what sort of person is revealed. There are all kinds of ways of asserting oneself. Lust need not always be the mere expression of sexual drives; indeed, much of the misuse of sex probably has little to do with lust. After all, many sexual sins fall under the headings of violence or infidelity. But the urge to dominate is the obvious drive of one on the attack, and this manifests itself in subtle ways.

There are the obvious, crass acts of the bully, but there are also the attempts to control made by the meek. There are the times when one deprived of an opportunity in her/his own life attempts to take vengeance on the world by thwarting another. There are the claims to know what is best for a loved one, when what is sought is domination of the other, not their flourishing.

And there is the lust which is assertion. Attacking means denying the urge to love, but the love that is associated with the physical cannot be denied. There is pride which denies the need to be loved, but the needs associated with physical companionship cannot be denied. And so lust is there as a substitute. Dominating others and denying one's own needs are ways of asserting oneself, of attacking the world around.

In national monuments and the way people decorate their homes, in the designer labels and the frequently renewed interiors, in the purchase of books to mark a snobbish status and in cars to proclaim wealth, people and groups continue to attack with the sin of gluttony. Again, there are the obvious kinds of gluttony, over-indulgence in food and drink. These acts of gluttony can be forms of attack, in the attempt to show off the ability to drink a lot, for example and so buttress one's self-assertion. But they can be refined. Is it pride or gluttony when a man looks down his nose at cheap wine but will spend much more on a bottle of a "good vintage"? The extravagant use of resources to gain a pleasure extrinsic to the resources themselves is gluttony, even if the resources do not go down one's throat.

And the attack can be directed. It might seem that any attack has to be directed, but that is not always the case. We are thinking of growth, still, and that can take these grotesque forms, these attacking ways, without direction. There can be a striking out in all directions just for the sake of it. Such attacking is straightforward, perverse self-assertion. Yet once one says, "I ought to have that," once envy creeps in, then there is direction. One can no longer love the person envied as one ought, and therein lies the sin – for this is no longer a case of greed or gluttony. It is claiming that someone else is in the wrong position, too high a position. Here we can recognize how easy it is for sin to pluck on sin. "Do you really envy him *that*? Surely, you won't let a little thing like that worry you." And so attention is focussed on the object not the person, and envy is avoided by appealing to – pride! And from this pride can come the dismissal of the real achievements of another, or the refusal to rejoice with them in their good fortune.

When objects are the focus of desire rather than people the focus of hatred, then we have avarice, and this can be an obvious form of attack. The pleasure lies not in consumption but in mere possession, the forcing of one's power or wealth or talents on the attention of others. The glutton may ultimately be floored or exhausted by one pleasure, but the miser has no pleasure except the contemplation of access to pleasure never to be enjoyed.

Then anger might seem to be the most obviously aggressive sin, the sin most easily associated with attacking, yet it takes different forms. There is the anger that builds on envy, but that differs from the anger that drives lust.

Again, anger (like pride) is a matter of valuing something wrongly. A lot is said about righteous anger, but most people know what is proper passion about a wrongful situation and what is simply self-assertion (even when it hides behind some justification in terms of zeal for the poor or hatred of tyranny). A passionate urge to remedy an evil will not simply end in anger. If the anger is all that is left, then there was no righteousness there to begin with. And the anger can go in several directions. All sin is ultimately destructive of the sinner, but anger is probably more obviously so, for there are times when it is simply aimed at oneself directly. Probably most of us have felt those twinges of anger with ourselves which really come as a result of pride. The real shame which can work repentance has little to do with this because there is no place for any pride ("You've let yourself down here") in it. Instead, we berate ourselves in much the same way as parents berate their children for swearing in front of a maiden aunt – not for swearing, not even for upsetting the aunt, but for letting down the parents.

Of course, the anger can also be directed at others. Again, it can be mixed with pride. Someone does not measure up to my expectations (why should they?) so I am angry. I am made to appear in a less than favourable light by some circumstance or even the failure of something mechanical, so my pride leads to anger. Even a tin-opener or the key on the side of a tin of corned beef can be the occasion of hurt pride – unless the situation is saved by laughter.

Of all the sins, one might think that sloth would be the last to be associated with attacking. But when sloth manifests itself as carelessness, it *is* a form of attack. Such thoughts as "I don't need to bother about doing this ..." can be an expression of pride when to do that thing is a matter of courtesy or is for the sake of someone else. Another kind of attacking self-assertion is when it is assumed that my indisputably great value will be perceived by all and there is no need for me to put myself out to impress others! Sloth here is joined with pride. Again, sloth can be a way by which one attacks oneself: one can begin with a low estimate of oneself and conform down to that.

But also there is sloth when one accepts a partial picture of oneself as a complete picture. In the gospel, the rich fool (Luke 12:13–21) might well be seen as guilty not so much of avarice as of sloth because he is prepared to be careless about a large part of life. He sees himself as the advertisers would like to portray all of us. Similarly, the parable of the demon and the demons (Luke 11:24–26) is about carelessness. And, arguably, it is, perhaps, a very modern kind of carelessness. As people have lost the idea that there may be a purpose for their lives that is not of their choosing, so a spiritual vacuity has arisen. All manner of influences can prey on people so that, well educated, kept fit in the gym, uncriticized by parent or teacher, superior to, even if passively compliant with, the demands of others, they are free in the sense of being at the disposal of whatever comes along.

Don't beat the air

The difficult question of purpose has just been mentioned. If growth is a natural and God-willed matter, and sin is a form of perverted or disordered growth, how do we grow aright? Here the positive forms of self-examination derived from the Bible can help, and perhaps especially that based on the fruit of the Spirit. For where the growth is wrong, it is growth not directed by and towards God but "growth" rooted and routed away from Him.

But also here something fundamental about the process of self-examination comes into play. I may be disturbed by or ashamed at some particular sin. Pride attacks when that sin becomes the be-all and end-all of my self-examination and my moral effort, for then I am laying down my own standard of perfection: "I would be perfect were it not for …". Rather, I should see that imperfection as evidence of my imperfection and be ready for a more thorough process of repair. I might be quite pleased with myself if I did overcome a particular temptation, but that doesn't mean that I am closer to God. And the pride I feel at overcoming that temptation might only serve to distance me further from Him.

If we are made by God, then it is reasonable to look for our purpose in Him, and that takes us back to the old-fashioned view, shared by Catholics and Protestants, that our purpose, the end for which we are created, is the praise of God issuing from the love of God. Our thoughts, words and deeds, then, are to be judged by how well they conform and conform us to that end.

And so we come to a few questions

Do I bother about why I do things?

Do I distinguish between doing things for a purpose and doing things for the sake of incidental benefits that may accrue as a result of my doing them?

Are there people for whom I prefer to do things? Why?

Do I distinguish between being keen to excel and being ambitious?

If the various parts of life were seen as events in an athletics meeting, in which event would I be doing best? How do I decide whether or not to be glad about that?

Do I compare myself with other people?

Do I compare my fortune in life with other people's?

Do I compare myself with Mother Teresa, for example?

A vagrant?

A new-comer to my church?

Where do I waste time?

What about energy?

What about resources?

Some work on the Bible

Read Genesis 4:1–16.

God does not reject Cain's sacrifice because of any failing on his part, but Cain is angry just at the way the world is. Who is my Abel?

Read Luke 15:11–32.

What is the elder son's mistake?

Read Matthew 25:31–46.

How would the King react if one of the goats apologized? Frame such an apology.

3. Defence

From the outside in

A question which is meant to plague people to-day is *Who am I?* The short answer once might have been, "Look at the label on your shirt." The chain store Marks and Spencer confused things here by using *St. Michael* as its brand label. Such advice could lead a reader to delusions of grandeur! If, however, such problems are avoided, you probably had the right name.

Somehow, that approach to the problem does not seem to appeal. We gain our identity and locate ourselves in the world by the various networks of relationships in which we are involved. And we can feel tensions between these networks. Thus, there can be conflicts between the claims of family and the claims of work. We can want to be loyal to friends, but if our friends fall into two groups we may wonder how we can be loyal to both sets.

From early days we are encouraged to seek approval, and certainly, the child who has never received approval can be seriously damaged. But this need can continue in different ways. We seek the approval of superiors because that is the way to success at work. We seek the approval of loved ones, often through their 'positive feed-back', not only because we cynically see that as the way of getting what we want from the relationship but also because we genuinely want to do the best for them, and so we need the reassurance that comes from knowing that we are loving them effectively. We seek the approval of friends because we value their friendship and because we need to belong, to know that we are not mad to think the way we think or value the activity we value, whether it be a matter of supporting a political party or going train-spotting. All these kinds of affirmation contribute to helping us think that our lives have not been wasted. Some may say they do not need the endorsement or approval of others, but most of us ask at some point whether we have wasted our time and usually we want something more than that, we want to feel appreciated.

Usually, we go beyond this need. Part of growing up is learning to enjoy things because we enjoy them, not because we win our parents' approval by engaging in their favourite activity or because we can win the approval of a gang by listening to the same music. We learn to say for ourselves why we think in a particular way or hold a certain point of view. This is the step, for example, from voting for a party "because my father voted that way and his father before him" to understanding what the party stands for and entering into a dialogue with the party. We also look for approval not from others but from *ourselves*. We begin to value our *integrity* even though we still value *integration*, and we strive to balance the two.

Nevertheless, we should not despise or lose sight of the external. We do not have all the answers inside ourselves, and we have been receiving, drawing in, for a long time, even since before ever we were aware of ourselves as individual human beings. The idea that there is some underlying I – the real person who has to be discovered – can be misleading and give rise to unnecessary anxiety. In other words, DNA has to work within a social setting.

In certain African tribes, there was no use of the death penalty. Instead, an offender was simply sent into exile. Though he had survival skills (for the level of existence was so basic that all tribal members could gather food and provide shelter for themselves), the exile would fade and die. The one exiled, like all the members of the tribe, only had life in the context of their relationships. In the Old Testament, there are several instances of identity being more than just a matter of *individual* identity. Families and clans suffer for the crime of one; blessings are inherited which are the reward of a particular ancestor. Similarly, the worship of God is the responsibility of a family even when it is the duty laid on one member in particular. And the continuation of family is seen as a responsibility laid on the individual, but also a means by which the individual gains status or identity. And in modern society, we still encounter tribalism of a sort just below the surface, and there we still value family loyalty. Not only is the concern of parents different from the interest of outsiders but violence within a family is seen as having an added dimension of horror.

Quite simply, we can see each person starting as a blank space which is to be shaped and defined by relationships and gradually acquiring the ability to build as well as the capacity for being built on. That way of viewing people is not as dismissive as it sounds because the building begins with the work of God. If we see ourselves as God's building site, and other people and situations as the tools and materials He uses, our supposed individuality and autonomy may take a knock, but we are led to an understanding of how God shapes people – as He shaped Abraham and his descendants individually, and the people of Israel as a whole through the Exodus and wilderness experience and through their tumultuous history.

At the same time ...

Partly because we need relationships for our own survival, we accept the place of acting. It is interesting to note that we think the *person* is important, yet the word *person* comes from the Latin word for a mask. The mask, the *persona*, was worn by an actor to indicate the character he was playing. It was that mask through which the actor spoke. (*Personare* means to sound through).

This acting is not always a bad thing. Children begin by following instructions before they can understand them, but they gradually internalize them and grow into the mask by which they can be recognized and with which they can function in society. When entering strange company, we often put parts of ourselves aside in order to be open to others and avoid causing needless offence. We also use masks to test how far we may trust those with whom we are mixing before we begin to talk about things that matter to us or points on which we are vulnerable. There is what might be called the superficial mask, which is not a deliberate falsification but does not reveal much of oneself. It both defends one and makes possible the gradual process of building communication with another person, another human being. There can be something overwhelming about the man or woman who is a stranger but who begins an encounter with some dramatic revelation about himself or herself.

But this use of masks can also be harmful. We know what it means to say someone is "two-faced"! We feel uneasy when we are manoeuvred into saying something, perhaps out of tact, that we do not feel is wholly what we believe. There can also be a sense of our own frailty that puts us at a disadvantage, if that is the right word, when dealing with others. This is well described by W.H. Auden. He writes;

> … we can hardly avoid thinking that the majority of persons we meet have stronger characters than we. We cannot observe others making choices; we only know what, in fact, they do, and how, in fact, they behave. Provided their actions are not criminal, their behaviour not patently vicious, and their performance of their job in life reasonably efficient, they will strike us as strong characters. But nobody can honestly think of himself as a strong character because, however successful he may be in overcoming them, he is necessarily aware of the doubts and temptations that accompany every important choice.[1]

We develop defence strategies partly because the world does not allow us to acknowledge our thoughts completely or own our weaknesses and partly because of the competitiveness which is a result of being conditioned by the quest for approval. Sometimes, because we have 'taken on board' so much of the world's ways of thinking, we cannot even acknowledge these weaknesses to ourselves.

Ministry of defence, not minister of grace

Sometimes these strategies impinge more on us than on others. We make a joke out of a serious situation, maybe even out of some sin that we have committed or some less than amiable characteristic we display. The mean man who never buys a drink feels he can get away with his meanness by jokingly boasting; the cruel man who mistreats his wife protects himself and avoids facing the harm he causes by making jokes at the expense of women; the man who has not achieved the success he thinks he deserves makes dismissive jokes about the more successful. Is this a manifestation of pride? Or is it the manifestation of the sloth which leads to the attitude of "There is nothing wrong with me, nothing I need to alter"?

Another defence strategy is to rewrite the past. On some occasion one shows less than full courage. In the evening, when reflecting on the day, one thinks, "How superior I showed myself to be by rising above that little man," when the truth is that the little man was your boss or an important client or a bullying director or governor who could make life very unpleasant. Yet pride prevents a confrontation with the truth, even in the privacy of one's own thoughts in one's own sitting room.

Again, envy, which might seem to be an aggressive sin because it springs from the perception that someone has something one does not have oneself, can also be defensive when it leads to defensive comparisons which say, "It's unfair – he had a better education/ a smoother manner/ more skill at golf/ Freemasonry/ he wasn't a Freemason/ he'd been to a public school/ he had been with the firm longer ..." Injustice does happen, but there is often a temptation to look away from our own shortcomings or even from those things which are not wrong but simply mean that someone else is more suited to a post or more deserving of some benefit or will derive greater benefit from and bestow greater benefit by reason of some good they receive. Envy here is about misplaced comparison, and it has to do with defending oneself by finding a point of comparison which is irrelevant or simply false. It is chastening to remember that envy is about one's *disposition*, not necessarily about the way the world is. It is therefore possible to be envious when there is nothing to envy.

And close kin to envy is anger. By "carrying the war into the enemy camp" I can assert myself. I defend myself against another by nursing anger, and I justify the anger in all sorts of ways. Yet even if there has been genuine injustice and hurt, the anger can take on a life of its own. The original offence is lost to sight, and the person, not her/his action, becomes the focus of attention, or I refuse to hear anything in defence or mitigation of the harmful action. To defend myself, I have to block out all rational analysis of the situation and strike out at anyone. By anger I divert attention from myself and fix blame on the circumstances or on another person. It is even possible to create an atmosphere of blame when there was not one previously. Something goes wrong, so I feel embarrassed or feel that I need to defend myself. Then I resent the situation in which I feel forced to take unjustified blame. Even though no one is blaming me, I may still feel blamed; I may even, through pride, blame myself. The resentment of this blame is transferred as anger on to someone else or on to anyone who dares ask a question about what has happened.

If anger seems at first an odd form of defence, the remaining three capital sins can also be deceptive. To see gluttony as defensive is not just to talk about "comfort eating"! Mere consumption, of anything, can be reassuring: it proves power and it keeps us from having truly to engage with anyone else. An extravagance, on clothes or books or theatre tickets, can be a way of asserting an identity which is not touched by the perceived blow. Thus, for example, by consuming in an extravagant way or by the exercise of lust, one is asserting control, control of resources or of another person. Such consumption entails subordinating the claims of justice, which might call for discipline or self-renunciation, to the defensive striking out from oneself. And the mere process of consumption without consideration of its impact on others, the very indulgence of lust, provides ways of ignoring the humanity of others. Lust becomes a substitute for love as does gluttony – in both, one is evading the challenges to love another and to grow oneself by looking for that which is more truly loveable in oneself. These two sins are about protection, defence, as they are about protecting us from the vision of ourselves as vulnerable because, once we see another as needing love, we see how we have failed in loving, and we are confronted at the same time with that need in ourselves. And then we are led to the acknowledgement of our incompleteness. Is the gourmet substituting the pleasure of eating for the communion of justice? Are some of the "lads" who put it about or consumers of pornography simply refusing to see others as people, substituting an assertive but immature wish to control for a response to the summons of love? They are defending a weak or fearful self from the challenge to grow, they are holding on to the child part of their nature when they need to grow as partners. In both cases, lust and gluttony, the practitioners are seeking to defend themselves from the claims of humanity – others' and their own. This is very different from delight in creation or the true enjoyment of sexual pleasure.

And balancing such aggressive forms of defence is avarice. It might seem that avarice has to do with acquisitiveness and so would be itself aggressive, yet the miser's pleasure lies in possession rather than acquisition. To acquire demands effort and may stimulate to virtue, as someone works to provide for others and himself/herself. That kind of labour is not avaricious and does not fall under the heading of acquisitiveness because it is the proper activity of any adult. Avarice comes in when possessions possess, when acquisition is not for use but for security - and not such security as saving for a home, but the spurious security of control by self-indulgence. *Use* has a broad sense here – there is a right use of a work of art, but there is also a debasing possessiveness with respect to works of art.

Avarice is very much, then, in this respect a matter of defence. The miser is secure, needing no one else and trusting in the idol of her/his possessions. The miser can look down on others, can claim to be richer than anyone else in the club. The expression "I can buy any man in the club-house" has been heard. But avarice and pride combine here. There is crude pride in possessions, but there can be a pride in the possession of talents which has nothing to do with joy in their use. It is simply a way of asserting, "I have this which, by common consent, is valued, and I have it in a greater degree than usual." Again, the miser is using a debased and debasing image of humanity because life is more than food and the body is more than clothes and the soul more than degrees.

In God we trust – everyone else pays cash

That heading, incorporating the American motto, is found in more than one bar in the U.S.A.. It contains both a symptom of the situation and its remedy.

If we think back to our own growing, we can remember times when we have felt let down by other people or by life itself. That is covered by the *everyone else pays cash* part of the heading. We learn the practice of defensiveness, and it becomes a habit. And the habit of defensiveness can lead to the habit of suspicion, and that can so influence our ways of relating that bad expectations become self-fulfilling. We even apply this grid in thinking about God.

We can pretend to be loving. We might say, "I'll do this because it is 'the loving thing to do', but I expect to be hurt by it." All the difference lies between *expect that* and *accept that I might*. And it is in accepting that we might be hurt that the way of love is opened, for it is the way of God with His human creatures. God is not defensive, and only by not being defensive can He enable people to grow and to love. God accepted that He might be hurt. This is part of the significance of such verses as 1 Peter 1:18–20:

> For you know that it was not with perishable things such as silver or gold that you were redeemed from the empty way of life handed down to you from your forefathers, but with the precious blood of Christ, a lamb without blemish or defect. He was chosen before the creation of the world, but was revealed in these last times for your sake.

Revelation 13:8 is also relevant:

> … the book of life belonging to the Lamb that was slain from the foundation of the world.

Or we can become self-deprecating to the point of cutting ourselves off from God. A good portrayal of this comes in Evelyn Waugh's *Unconditional Surrender*. The scene in 1943. as Guy Crouchback, a Roman Catholic temporary officer in the Royal Corps of Halberdiers, attends his father's funeral:

> *I'm worried about you,"* his father had written in the letter which, though it was not his last … Guy regarded as being in a special sense the

conclusion of their regular, rather reserved correspondence of more than thirty years. His father had been worried, not by anything connected with his worldly progress, but by his evident apathy ...

Guy's prayers were directed to, rather than for, his father. For many years now the direction in the *Garden of the Soul*, "Put yourself in the presence of God,' had for Guy come to mean a mere act of respect, like signing the Visitors' Book at an Embassy or Government House. He reported for duty saying to God: 'I don't ask anything from You. I am here if You want me. I don't suppose I can be any use, but if there is anything I can do, let me know,' and left it at that.

'I don't ask anything from You'; that was the deadly core of his apathy; his father had tried to tell him, was now telling him. That emptiness had been with him for years now even in his days of enthusiasm and activity in the Halberdiers. Enthusiasm and activity were not enough. God required more than that. He had commanded all men to *ask*.

In the recesses of Guy's conscience there lay the belief that somewhere, somehow, something would be required of him; that he must be attentive to the summons when it came. They also served who only stood and waited. He saw himself as one of the labourers in the parable who sat in the market-place waiting to be hired and were not called into the vineyard until late in the day. They had their reward on an equality with the men who had toiled since dawn. One day he would get the chance to do some small service which only he could perform, for which he had been created. Even he must have his function in the divine plan. He did not expect an heroic destiny. Quantitative judgements did not apply. All that mattered was to recognise the chance when it offered.

The idea that God has a task for us is frightening, and yet the acceptance of that idea can dispel the sins that come from defensiveness. If I have no purpose, I can easily think I have no value. (The two are not always linked, but they tend to be.) If others define my purpose, I fall prey to their expectations, and so I need defence mechanisms. If I am left to define my own purpose, I need to defend it and I can easily be in the position described by Auden, of seeing others apparently confident and strong as compared to me who have nothing with which to vindicate my purpose except such reasonings as I can scrape together, which will appear sometimes stronger, sometimes weaker. In this situation, defensiveness comes in again.

To trust in God is to start to look beyond self. It is to accept vulnerability, but also to recognize that one does not have anything that needs defending on one's personal account. And it requires as fundamental the belief that God does not need defending. This is necessary to save us from the use of God as one of our own weapons of defence. "I cannot let you get away with that because it is blasphemy," – that statement can, on occasion, not always, be more a reflection of feeling threatened than of any true love of God. Might we not better begin in the following way, "I am hurt by your saying or doing that because I share the pain of the

God Who loves you"? Might that not be part of the meaning of Colossians 1:24?

Questions, questions ...

What experiences have I had that have been uplifting?
Do I recall these with gratitude?
Do I seek to grow from them or to go back to them?
Do they give me life, or do I disparage the present by looking back to them?

Am I protective of any relationship? or am I possessive of it?
Can I distinguish between these two attitudes?

Do I find it easier to love the starving in Africa than to love people in the local shops?

If someone talks about me, what do I like them to say?
How do I get them to say it?

Are there people of whom I like to hear bad reports?
Is there a particular kind of gossip I enjoy?
Are there particular sins I like to hear about?

Are there things precious to me that I should feel silly talking about? Why?

Are there things of importance in my life that I should feel embarrassed to talk about?
Am I interested in such things in the lives of others? Why?

Who knows me?
Who knows what I enjoy?

Who knows what I value?
Who knows what I fear?

How often do I open my heart to God?

Is my prayer a matter of "saying prayers," or is it an honest conversation?

Do I ever deny wanting something? Why?

Am I more keen to be successful or frightened of failing?
What counts as success in life?
And what counts as failure?

Some work on the Bible

Read 1 Kings 10:14–11:13.
Solomon sought security by becoming "one of the crowd," by becoming like other kings.
He had all the trappings of earthly power.
What do I admire in others?
And what do I envy?
On what would I base any claim to status?

Read Jeremiah 36.
Jehoiakim seems to be asserting strength, but he is also fearful of his courtiers.
How big a part does denial play in my life?
Do I listen to the traditional sources of guidance?
And what happens when I don't like what they say?

Read Matthew 25:14 – 30.
Do I deny or fail to see what I do have because I envy what others have?
Do I believe that in God's sight any tasks are small?
Do I take any risks in my life with God?
in my moral thinking?
in my use of resources?

How do I deny responsibility?

Do I think "I can't be valued"? 'Quantitative judgements do not apply'

4. Problems on the Way

The barking dogs in the night

The grouping of actions under the two headings of attack and defence might seem a reasonable way of looking at sins, but there is a danger that any action might be put under one or other of those headings! Did you do that good deed in order to impress (attack), or did you do it to make up for some failure in the past (defence)? It would be possible to apply the same questioning to all actions, and that can lead to cynicism about oneself and others, a doubting of all actions which is caused by a doubting of all motives.

This point has to be accepted. We certainly do need to be alert to the dangers of self-deception and hypocrisy and we need to look at how we achieve that consistency which is proper and healthy integrity. But the danger of cynicism, about oneself or others, is very real, and we live in a cynical age. Think of how police officers are often portrayed on television. We expect the police to be cautious because they are dealing with people categorized from the start as suspects, and so as calling for a measure of scepticism in the reception of their words and the assessment of their actions. But many of the characters we see on our television screens and in real life have taken that approach too thoroughly, and everything is brought down to its basest interpretation.

Indeed, the possibility of someone's behaving honestly, for good reasons, for the right reason is discounted.

The habit of cynicism leads to a habit of distrust. (The Cynics were a group of philosophers whose name means 'dog-like'.) Under these circumstances, people say that the accounts of no charity are to be trusted because accountants will find ways around; no politician speaks the truth; no paper is reliable; no reporting is dependable. These blanket condemnations mean that the cynic views the world as living on a web of lies. It is an impregnable position because anything offered in defence of the target can be dismissed as coming from an equally unreliable source. Unfortunately, if everyone is to be seen as a liar, which is what this position implies, one has to turn the same judgement on oneself, for one's mind is stocked with what has come from the outside, from the world of lying and deceit and baseness.

This is to paint the portrait in vivid colours, but the caricature works because the lines of the truth can be seen in it. But what is to save us from this position of cynical doubt?

First, very simply, we can look at the action or thought under scrutiny and ask whether, in itself, it fulfilled a moral rule or duty. If so, it has a basic claim to be innocent. We accept that our motives are often mixed, but that does not absolve us from the responsibility of acting in accordance with the best moral guidance available to us, and that guidance is usually about actions. In the parable of the Pharisee and the tax-collector (Luke 18:9-14) no fault is found with the actions of the Pharisee. He ought to have done what he did.

Akin to this is the question of whether something is morally permissible. In itself, that should re-assure, but care is needed. To have one drink may be morally permissible, but it is not right to say that, because an individual drink is permitted, having ten individual drinks is permitted! When the issue is not one of fulfilling a duty but of exercising a freedom, context (it may be permissible to do this, but is it appropriate?) and habit or accumulated effect need to be borne in mind. It may be permissible to do something, such as play a game or watch a television programme, but if the accumulated effect of playing the game is the development of a compulsion or the accumulated effect of watching a particular television programme is to mould one's behaviour, then caution is needed.

Together, these considerations lead to a third answer to this problem. As was said, our actions are often from mixed motives. But if we may invoke once more the medical analogy, the exercise of self-examination is not about treating symptoms. Our concern must be with the whole condition. So we need to look for patterns. The question that needs to be asked of oneself may not so much be *What was my motive in that situation?* but *What moves me to actions of that sort?* A series of actions can be seen as displaying a pattern. This is where the law alone is not enough because, by its nature, it will deal with individual events.

There are three outcomes to that type of question about patterns. First, there is the person who does not scrutinize motives. Ideally, we should all become like that because we should not need to doubt our motives. But until that blissful state is reached, the one who does not scrutinize or is not alert to motives must either be considered blessed in simplicity (and that may be part of the meaning of *Blessed are the pure in heart*) or they need to begin looking at motives to avoid the attitude of the Pharisee in the parable.

Secondly, there are those who do look at their motives and find nothing wrong. If that is an honest and truthful assessment, they must give thanks to God for what has been achieved through them and in them. That can sound like the opening of the Pharisee's prayer – "God, I thank you that I am not …." But such a thanksgiving can also prevent pride. But they must also be ready for surprises, for the time of seeing things in a new light and learning that perhaps they did not know themselves as well as they thought.

This is where examination of the process of self-examination is important. Always using the same method can stop us from becoming aware of parts of ourselves we need to confront.

Thirdly, there are those who look at their motives and are worried. If for the satisfied the words *our motives are usually mixed* are a warning, for such people as these they can be a comfort. This is not because they must resign themselves to never getting things right but because they can see themselves as on the way. The correcting of motives can be done partly through looking at the purposes of an action or class of actions. *Where is my service of God in this?* is a useful question. But again, people may fool themselves into thinking that they are seeking to serve God in all their actions. Therefore, to make a conscious offering of an action *before* doing something, rather than having a broad sense of doing things as a Christian, can begin to work on motives. This is not because it replaces the motives; rather, it is because it sanctifies the action. Whatever may lurk deep down inside, such an offering can make of the very deed an act of repentance, of looking again. Muscles and nerves in a limb can be damaged and a leg may not function properly. The approach of medicine can in such cases be to exercise the whole limb so that the system is 're-educated'. Something like that is envisaged here, so that the deed becomes key and concentration on that means the rest of the system can learn.

And this may help those who will always worry, those who can never let go of that damaging sense of unworthiness that is not mock modesty but is nearer to neurosis. They need to hear that they are accepted and that such offering of their actions is part of the process by which their acceptance by God is affirmed. In this way, they can come to accept themselves.

How miserable a sinner are you?

In the General Confession in the Church of England's Book of Common Prayer we describe ourselves as miserable sinners. In fact, part of the problem with sin is that it seems to make people happy. The talk of attack and defence seems to be an attempt to explain it and to refuse to accept that one sins because one enjoys that particular sin.

Here, the rules can help, but only as we seek reasons for the rules. Does a moral rule lead to human flourishing? If so, it can give a reason why that particular sin is to be avoided.

A much-debated issue in moral thinking is the problem of weakness of will. How can anyone knowingly do what is wrong? So stated, the answer easily comes back "Because they enjoy it." But the trouble with knowing that you ought to do something is that if you really mean that, ought to do it – the word *ought* moves it to the top of one's priorities. We ought to do what we ought to do, and there is no gainsaying that.

Perhaps we can begin by thinking of an example outside the realm of morality and think of competing pleasures. If somebody has limited money and has to choose between two pleasures, both permissible, how is s/he to choose? The choice of one will make the other unattainable. Yet this does not really explain things because what one ought to do might not be pleasant. To choose what is pleasant but wrong over what is right but unpleasant is surely understandable and a very common experience.

First, one can be schooled so as to see the right as pleasant – or at least as what one ought to desire. This again is where the achievement of human flourishing and the safeguarding of integrity and integration have a part to play. My behaviour is part of the life of a wider community, so integration has to be guarded, but it is also part of the story of my life, so integrity, being able to live with myself, should also be guarded. It is the losing sight of these aspects of behaviour that goes some way toward explaining how people can do what they know to be wrong. Here, also, the much-maligned rules can be helpful. Part of the schooling that we need comes through the obedience to rules. A craftsman may do instinctively something that produces the right result, a beautiful piece of furniture, for example. And the craftsman may even be incapable of explaining how he has managed to do so, but he has served an apprenticeship, internalised the rules of his craft, and so become proficient. "Do you want to produce a beautiful life?" might here be a better question than, "Do you want to do this?" The internalising of rules can help in the formation of the skill which is displayed in good deeds. The rules can guide one toward the real aim. Of course, there is a need for revision and refinement, for criticism of systems and of those responsible for administering them. Blind obedience has its dangers, but so does the attitude that says one must work everything out for oneself.

So, secondly, we might think of distinguishing between believing that one would enjoy doing something and wanting to do it. There are various wrong acts that one might say one would enjoy – from punching the a neighbour to sleeping with his wife – but one does not want to do … and not only for the non-moral reason that the neighbour is bigger. To develop the right kind of wanting is part of the training in life that Christianity offers. Yes, I sin just because I enjoy it, but as the quest for becoming a whole person continues, so the avoidance of what erodes that wholeness becomes more of a priority. I might ask myself, *Does my wanting something prevent my seeking at the same time the kingdom of God?*

He'll with three giants fight

We have already come across the writer Mark the Ascetic. In the fifth century he wrote:

> Imagine that there are three powerful and mighty giants of the Philistines …
> when these three have been overthrown and slain, all the power of the demons is fatally weakened. These three giants are the vices already mentioned; ignorance, the source of all evils; forgetfulness, its close relation and helper; and laziness, which weaves the dark shroud enveloping the soul in murk.[1]

Although writers often try to analyse sin to see whether there is a chief one to which all others can be traced or to find what all sins have in common, this list of three seems odd. But Mark is not talking about specific sins; rather he is describing what creates the atmosphere in which sin can flourish. These three can help individual sins breed.

The imagery of the giant is not wholly misplaced. Atmospheres take on lives of their own, ignorance excuses ignorance, sloth with respect to one kind of activity spreads to other areas of life and forgetfulness leads to a general carelessness. And to use the imagery of fairy tales, if a giant stamps his foot, a house many miles away can be shaken. So, to begin with....

Sloth

The words from Mark the Ascetic come from a collection known as *The Philokalia*, probably the greatest work on prayer of the Eastern Church. The opening words of that collection catch one's attention. They come from a monk who probably wrote in the fifth century, and he says the following:

> There is among the passions an anger of the intellect, and this anger is in accordance with nature. Without anger a man cannot attain purity: he has to feel angry with all that is sown in him by the enemy.[2]

(It should be noted that the word *intellect* here is used in a somewhat wider sense than we normally use it.)

Our lives should be marked by a discontent which has nothing to do with blaming God or other people for our lot or for the state of the world. It is not the anger of a teenager who blames his parents for everything from Third World debt to the melting of the polar ice-caps. Rather, it is akin to the discontent of the lover who feels that whatever he does or says will be inadequate as a response to the sure and certain love given to him, lavished on him. It is like the dissatisfaction of the musician who knows that, however hard s/he may practise, the effort will never do justice to the work to be performed – in other words, the work which is more than the sum total of the notes on the page. It is like the straining of the artist who seeks to convey the object and her/his response to it through the paint and canvas yet knows there is still something inaccessible in the object and beyond the artist's powers of expression.

We go away from that discontent at our peril. It is not a matter of not having the energy to be discontent all the time because this is not an energy-wasting form of discontent. If anything, it is one that will make us focus our thinking and loving, our energies and resources with clearer priorities. It will deliver us from wastefulness.

This anger, however, this discontent can be hard because it turns us toward ourselves, sometimes as individuals, sometimes as groups, whether church, community or nation. So we find defences, as sloth generates excuses. We can say, "Not yet." Sloth hides the fear of change: whatever habit of sin we may have, whether that sin be pride or lust, anger or envy, we defend ourselves, and that defence is evidence of sloth. At times, sloth prevents us from turning away not from sin, but from positive growth in what is good. We become like the grumbling Israelites in the wilderness. Cynicism can stem from sloth. We might not want to be challenged by somebody's goodness, so we cast doubts upon it. We might think, that way has never been my way, so it cannot be the right way. And we show sloth not just in inaction, but also in not concentrating: what is really happening here? how am I called upon to act? We all know the person who does not pay attention when we talk to them but is already thinking of what they want to say or is looking over our shoulder at somebody else, literally or metaphorically.

This last type of sloth might be called the sloth of the modern age, which manifests itself, paradoxically, in frenetic activity. Society dare not ask itself, *What is the point?* or *What is truly valuable?* and so it hides in activity, too careless to face the challenge and task of its own correction. If we, society, church or individuals, could concentrate with this divine discontent, we would do a lot less but might achieve a lot more. The urge to get on with the next thing can be used to stop us from thinking about or preparing for the last things. And it is sloth that keeps us living on the surface, not going deeply into ourselves and our relationships with God or with other people.

Sloth is not just the sloth of the individual. There is sloth in society, sloth in averting our eyes from unpalatable truths or from facing changes that may demand sacrifice. This problem is well displayed in some of the journalism of Charles Dickens, but the twentieth century did not see an end of such sloth and it looks as though the twenty-first century will continue to be affected by it. The sloth of complacency or the sloth expressed in fear of increasing taxation, the failure of imagination to look for solutions that may demand change on the part of those who take it upon themselves to solve other people's problems, such manifestations of sloth hold back much good. G.K. Chesterton's words toll to warn us:

> From all that terror teaches,
> From lies of tongue and pen,
> From all the easy speeches
> That comfort cruel men,
> From sale and profanation
> Of honour and the sword,
> From sleep and from damnation,
> Deliver us, good Lord.

There is sloth in the Crucifixion. The sloth that resists challenge and the call to grow is shown by the priests. The sloth that is happy with the superficial and looks only for quick and easy answers is shown by the crowd. The sloth that evades responsibility and finds it easier not to notice another's humanity is shown by Pilate. The atmosphere of sloth has taken over, with the grinding of machinery (religious and political) whose operators, or rather minions, are afraid to question and powerless to halt it.

And we are warned by the Bible's example of Egypt to escape the sloth of relying on power and the wonders of what we see around us or of retreating into the slavery that is content with having enough to eat and ignores the call to go out into the wilderness to meet God. If it was fear or envy, avarice or anger that led to the Crucifixion of Jesus, it was the sloth of the world that created the situation in which that could happen. And Jesus came to wake us.

Ignorance

In the ordinary course of things, law courts work on the principle that ignorance of the law is no excuse. This is an obvious safeguard against the possibility of defendants' claiming they did not know stealing was illegal, for example. It is a reminder that engaging in certain activities brings responsibilities. For example, although the general public may not know all the law relating to transport, if one works in the transport industry, one has a responsibility to know and abide by the relevant laws. Of course, no ordinary citizen can be expected to know all the laws of the land, or even where to find them. But even if ignorance were acceptable as an excuse in some cases, we should be shocked if someone were to plead, "I didn't know it was against the law to murder/rape/steal/assault." Such a person would either be psychiatrically abnormal or just desperate.

Yet we fall into this way of reacting when we make excuses on the grounds of ignorance, and such ignorance is a sign of a lack of love. Love makes us sensitive, and such sensitivity is a form of knowledge. Love would make one careful, careful about justice and careful for the individual with whom one is dealing, and such care would be a form of prudence, which is a kind of knowledge, knowledge which is more about knowing *how* than knowing *facts*.

We tend to put knowledge before love (one can only love what one knows) but all the most important knowledge – the knowledge that grows in relationships, the knowledge that is a true appreciation of an artwork or piece of music, the knowledge that puts us in tune with nature and does not just open up new ways of exploiting it – all this knowledge is the fruit of love, and there is an ignorance which is the result of a lack of love.

Just as knowledge can lead to the development of habits, so can ignorance. We settle down to a way of life that is shaped by the limits of our knowledge, shaped by our ignorance. Our ignorance blunts our perception of what is happening and we love the darkness rather than the light … perhaps because we do not want our lack of love to be exposed, the lack of that love which seeks to spread itself, to explore where and how to love. We come back to defence, to wanting not to be hurt or having to grow. Perhaps the best exposition of this is the Bette Middler ballad "The Rose".

Here ignorance is more than the sum of what people do not know. Just as there can be received knowledge, so there can be received, institutional ignorance. Areas of ethical concern or pastoral delicacy can be ignored by the medical machinery; the agony of the individual can be ignored by the moralising panoply of the church; what 'stands to reason' can be agreed upon in a pub. In these instances, further thought is ruled unnecessary. Was not the Nazi war-effort serviced by scientists and technicians of great ability? Yet they were not wise despite all their cleverness. They chose a path of ignorance.

Here is a spiritual giant needing to be challenged so that growth in knowledge, sometimes painful and unsettling, can take place. This growth is necessary on the way to true repentance. A pall of distraction or excuses can be thrown over a situation which is really a turning from reality (and so is a form of ignorance). Paradoxically, it is a form of ignorance that masks ignorance. Such pleas as reasons of state, keeping people happy, keeping the peace, reverence for long-established forms and holding the family together can save us from confronting what is happening.

We choose ignorance in various ways, often in drawing on false comfort. Consider the following turns of phrase: *I'd rather not think about* and *Don't let's talk about that* and *You'll be all right.* Though sometimes helpful, these can become evasions, options for ignorance. I see someone getting on the 'bus, so I look down into my book to avoid eye contact which might encourage her/him to sit next to me and pour out their troubles. Do I have to watch the news? What difference does one more suspected criminal executed in a foreign country make to me? "Is it nothing to you, all you who pass by?", in the centuries-old words from the Book of Lamentations, used by the church in Holy Week to evoke pity on the afflicted Jesus and echoing as a lament over the victims of Auschwitz or Rwanda?

Just as ignorance can spring from a lack of love, so it can be a seed-bed for other sins. Pilate, the priests and the crowd all had their sins, but each sin covered an area where sensitivity would have alerted them - and should alert us. As that area of sensitivity was closed over, so the area of ignorance increased and the scope for doing what was right was decreased. They failed to ask what was really going on, they failed in the humility that asks the questions *What if I am wrong?* and *What new truth might there be here?*

Yet the ignorance is not just a matter of ignorance of things or people "out there". We take it for granted that we know ourselves. At the temple of the oracle in Delphi the instruction 'Know yourself' was placarded. In Greek history and mythology, there are stories of people who sought advice from the oracle and were given an enigmatic answer but interpreted that answer in a way that suited themselves, only to fall into disaster. If you seek advice, can you cope with it? Can you trust yourself to examine the answer you receive in order to avoid being deceived into sorrow, even *self-deceived* into sorrow? Do you know what your temptation is when you receive this partially hidden knowledge?

The worst sort of ignorance is not ignorance of facts – after all, only God can know all. Nor is it even ignorance of the moral law, for we are growing and repentance is possible, while we have a Judge Who knows us well. It is not even straightforward ignorance of God, though we may use '*ignorance*' as a cover for rebellion. Ignorance of ourselves is the ground from which pride can grow, but a contemptuous cynicism can grow as well. Ignorance can lead to an inflated estimate of self or a God-denying dismissal of humanity, ourselves included. And we can be afraid of having that ignorance remedied.

Would Jesus have been crucified had the people known Who He was? That is to ask too much. But would He have been crucified had they known themselves? Jesus' teaching is a way of exploring and expanding self-knowledge in the light of God. How often in the gospels do we read of His using stories and leading the hearers into seeing where they are in the story? The hearer is being led to know herself/ himself. Can we bear that labour?

"What is truth?" said Pilate. "Father, forgive them for they know not what they do," said Jesus. Was Pilate arrogant or afraid? Are we ready to come to know what we do?

Forgetfulness

Accidents happen, but there is such a thing as driving without due care and attention. To forget to pick up the bread from the shop on an ordinary day is one thing, to forget a wedding anniversary is quite different. The forgetfulness that is the spiritual giant we have to confront is of the latter type in each case. It is a kind of carelessness and, like some forms of ignorance, it is the result of a lack of love. We can develop a habit of taking things or people for granted which brings with it a lack of gratitude, a failure to value. There can be a confidence in oneself or in the established ways, and a carelessness resulting from that confidence, carelessness as to whether the original purpose is being served creeps in. There can be failure to guard words and thoughts, and then a sinful habit gains acceptance as just 'part of my nature', until finally I become blind to its sinfulness.

Each of these failings is illustrated in the story of Israel in the Old Testament and each is echoed in the story of the Passion. In the liturgy of Good Friday, the passage known as the Reproaches can be seen as rebuking forgetfulness. But in the Old Testament, the prophets and the writers of the historical books take pains to remind Israel of what God has done for them – they have received but not responded. For Christians, all virtue can be summed up under the heading of gratitude because the good we do is always a response to the good God has done for us and to us. Our very ability to act is the result of God's action, calling us to respond. An action may be free, but that does not mean that it appeared from some independently existing well of goodness within the one who acts. I can ignore the call of God, go away from it, lose sight of it, and thus forgetfulness, a being adrift, takes hold. This happens at all levels: societies lose their moral anchorage; groups and clubs - and church congregations - change and become cliques. Churches see themselves as having a life and logic of their own, and individuals believe they should be the sole arbiters in all kinds of matters. Forgetfulness of how we are related to others, to God and to our world casts us adrift.

When Israel lost its gratitude, its awareness of dependence, it kept a form of religion, but that religion became a means of national identity and then an instrument of national idolatry, not a tool for national self-criticism. Many would see several societies and nations as now facing the same process. There is a forgetfulness of the standards of justice, truth, purity and love by which the Christian's walk with God is to be measured. And this has happened in the life of the church and the churches.

There is a forgetfulness that leads to an acceptance of spiritual flabbiness. If we remember our weakness, our incompleteness and our dependence, then we are led back to Christ, and He does not upbraid the weak but helps them. If we remember the greatness of our calling, we are made aware of the dignity that comes from a relationship with God, and so are stimulated to offer what is best, to work with that divine discontent which will always seek to do more. But when either of these is forgotten the result is either pride or depression. And when both are forgotten the result is Pontius Pilate. He had plenty of trappings around him and so was shielded from the vision of his own weakness. He could rely on power, not his own, but certainly not God's. He was sufficiently callous to be cynical about what the best of even pagan learning should have caused him to respect. Such figures re-appear in every walk of life.

In the General Thanksgiving in the Church of England's Book of Common Prayer, we give thanks for "the means of grace and the hope of glory." *Means of grace* can be interpreted in two ways: it can be understood as the means by which grace is obtained (as in the sacraments and the preaching of the Word), or as the means to achieve our end - that is grace itself, grace is the means. We need to remember both.

The opposite of forgetfulness, however, seems unrealistic. It you are in a monastery, it might be thought that, of course, you can remember God all the time, but surely we are not expected to, are we? First, we need to remember that we are limited. This means we cannot give the same kind of attention to several things at once. We may pray for our work before we start it and after we finish it, but some very practical words from Dorothy L. Sayers may also help. She wrote:

> … a building must be good architecture before it can be a good church … a painting must be well painted before it can be a good sacred picture; that work must be good work before it can call itself God's work … The official Church wastes time and energy, and, moreover, commits sacrilege, in demanding that secular workers should neglect their proper vocation in order to do Christian work - by which she means ecclesiastical work. The only Christian work is good work well done. [3]

More succinctly, there are the words in her translation of Dante's *Purgatory*: "To pray when one ought to be working is as much a sin as to work when one ought to be praying."[4]

More briefly, Aquinas remarks, in a slightly different context, that someone on a journey need not think every step of the way about the ultimate goal of the journey. The fact that a driver was praying would not excuse him if charged with driving without due care and attention. Perhaps God wants our lives, and prayer (as usually understood) is only one *part* of those lives.

Secondly, the question "Could I pray while doing this?" can help. This is not about whether I can divide my attention but whether I can welcome the presence of God in my mind at this point. If the answer is "No", I need to ask whether that is the case simply because of a need to concentrate. If so, the work can be offered to God. But if there is some other reason that makes me awkward about prayer I need to ask whether I ought to be doing whatever it is.

Thirdly, forgetfulness takes different forms. The words at the start of Psalm 70 can be a useful prayer: "O God, make speed to save me; O LORD, make haste to help me." These words can and should be prayed not only in times of obvious temptation, as when one is assailed by a besetting sin, such as the temptation to dwell on long-nursed anger or lustful thoughts, but also when one is tempted to pride or self-satisfaction, or when things are going well and we think we are in no danger. They are recommended for such use in a sermon from the early church. After travelling in the Middle East and experiencing monastic life in Bethlehem and Egypt, John Cassian founded two monasteries in the West in 415. He wrote two works based upon what he had learned in the East, and in one of these, *The Conferences*, he relates a sermon on this verse from Psalm 70.[5]

A classic tale illustrating the danger of forgetfulness is the story of Sir Balaam, told by Alexander Pope in his *Moral Essays*, Epistle III, lines 339–402. Balaam forgets the dictates and guidance of his faith as his wealth increases, and as he conforms more and more to the ways of the world into which he enters, so he is more and more corrupted. As a careful merchant he follows his faith and is

> A plain good man, and Balaam was his name;
> Religious, punctual, frugal, and so forth;
> His word would pass for more than he was worth.

But then Pope writes the following:

> The dev'l was piqued such saintship to behold,
> And longed to tempt him like good Job of old:
> But Satan now is wiser than of yore,
> And tempts by making rich, not making poor.

We need again to pray the prayer of the Book of Common Prayer's Litany: "In all time of our tribulation; *in all time of our wealth* ... ... Good Lord, deliver us." (The italics, not in the original, have been added by the writer.)

But remedying our forgetfulness can also increase our pleasure by heightening our concentration. *This task or encounter is God's gift to me*, or *I can bring it to God* – either of those thoughts adds a value and depth to the encounters, tasks and scenes of life.

The gospels were written with the benefit of hindsight. Much harm is done if we read the Passion narratives as though we were the official enquiry commission attempting to apportion blame. The story is both rooted in time and universal. We need to see ourselves through the lens of this story. Shall I forget the love of Christ and the impact of His call, turning away as Peter did? Shall I forget that I cannot get out of being human and relating to others as human? Shall I forget that when I relate to them as things I debase myself just as Pilate did? Above all, shall I forget the covenant of grace by which God has bound me to Himself through baptism into Christ, as the Jewish leaders failed in awareness of the covenant? Shall I forget the freedom to which I am brought by Jesus as the Passover lamb, and go back to the slavery of sin? Shall I slight the love of God by thinking that it is always there – and so I need not bother – rather than thinking that it is always there and so is always calling me?

Remember your manners

Something was said above earlier about ingratitude and how all sin is characterised by it. The proud man, were he grateful, would realize that he owes to others and to God whatever is the basis of his pride, and so, though he might still rejoice in his work or his achievements, there would come humility to counter pride. The glutton would learn through gratitude the right use of the goods s/he wastes, including the good of her/his own physical health. The envious would learn to distinguish between the rightful quest to excel, to do well whatever task is given, and the distracting carping about another's rewards, or could be led by gratitude to contentment with what s/he has and be delivered from that striving to possess which leads to avarice.

Just being grateful can strengthen a relationship. In marriage there are a right way and a wrong way of taking for granted. Of course, one should be able to rely upon one's partner, but that is not the same as treating her/him as a door-mat! Taking care to express gratitude and appreciation enables the other to know that, in the most precious of human relationships, s/he is "getting it right".

Even the simple practice of saying grace before a meal is a way of turning the ordinary things of daily life into something of sacramental value, as it gives us pause to remember God as *the* giver.

Nowadays there is an unwillingness to say "Sorry", but there is also, often, a reluctance to say "Thank you". To acknowledge that we are dependent upon others is no bad thing, for it can lead to joy: "How marvellous it is that I have the help of that person, that he or she troubles themselves about me!." And those sorts of thoughts, flowing from gratitude, can lead to an awareness of our own place in the chain of dependence, as we are alerted to the fact that others are dependent upon us.

Keeping out of trouble

One drawback of many of the 'sin lists' used for self-examination is that they are about things you should not do. "Thou shalt not" seems to be like a warning that alerts us to danger, like the warning by a railway line or a poison label on a bottle.

On the one hand, this may be liberating. To know that one is avoiding sin by observing prohibitions leaves a wide field open for actions which are not in themselves sinful. On the other hand, however, quite apart from the image of God as the strict parent or schoolmaster that such an expression of morality might encourage, there is the danger that one may think one is good just because one has observed these prohibitions.

A day spent doing pleasant, non-sinful, activities can be very enjoyable. Then it becomes a week, and then a lifetime. There are positive commands – love God and love your neighbour – and it is worth asking not only whether any of one's deeds this day has been unloving toward God or neighbour, but also to ask wherein has that love been apparent. What have I done to show my love of God and neighbour?

Even doing certain unpleasant tasks can cover this problem. "I've provided for my family," for example. Yes, and that is part of the deal; the work would have been there and would have had to be done whether or not you had a family, and doing what comes with having a family is not something praiseworthy but rather it is bad if you do not provide when you can.

Once again, the 'keeping-out-of-trouble' approach can lead to the view of human beings as having a private space in themselves or in their lives which is entirely theirs to do with as they will. It can also lead to an attitude to human life that makes of it the working of a robot, because it reduces the scope for response to the unusual. In the parable of the Good Samaritan, the first two men who walked past the victim in the road might well have been keeping themselves ritually pure so that they could fulfil their duties in the Temple.

But often human behaviour, and the morality that should shape it, need to be seen as arts rather than sciences.

Because thou art righteous shall there be no more cakes and ale?

That question of Sir Toby Belch should help us scrape the lingering seaweed of sin off the boat of our lives.

There can be a fear of joy that comes from the experience of pain and disappointment in the past or the wish still to make amends (as if one could). Christians can see all their praying as though it were nothing but the sending of postcards from the vale of tears. This is another form of cynicism, this time about the world rather than about oneself.

Sin involves us in denying the reality of other people. They have no place, no rights; they are here for me. Release from sin means that we can see people as real, in their pain and limitations, certainly, but as of the same flesh and blood as ourselves, as bound up in the one world with us. In the hymn "New every morning," we dedicate the day to God. In that hymn occur the lines

> Old friends, old scenes will lovelier be
> As more of heaven in each we see.

These words can help us see how there can be joy in the recovery of the normal, the ordinary in the balance of our lives and of the world.

And the same is true of pleasures. Once again, rules can be helpful. If an activity does not conflict with the moral law and you enjoy it, then get on and enjoy it. Self-examination might reasonably make us ask whether our lives have not been too confined. Of course, we must avoid the traps of thinking we are not having enough fun, or of thinking that if we are not happy in doing something it cannot be the right thing to be doing. Also, as was remarked earlier, there is a distinction to be drawn between the individual act that is permissible and the repeated act that may do harm (or the inappropriate act that may offend or be misunderstood). While happiness is not guaranteed, misery is not an infallible sign of virtue or correctness.

Jesus' call to people to receive the kingdom as a child may help us understand something of this. To embrace without fear what is good and joyful now is to grow. We should recall how Saint John writes that perfect love casts out fear, and as love grows, so the valuing of each moment can grow. This valuing of the moment is not about possessing and holding on to it, for that is impossible. The wish to hang on to moments can lead only to disappointment. The valuing in view here is about seeing and receiving the moment as a sacrament of eternity. This particular view, musical performance, sexual activity, celebration, moment of tranquillity, a smile or experience of being helped can be about the kingdom, and can even be sacraments of it – outward and visible signs of inward and spiritual grace.

"It's not my fault."

If you take the list of the seven capital sins, you can easily identify some sin or other that you have committed. You might say, "I was angry with that person"; "I envied him"; "I was proud about..."; "I over-indulged in that"; "I felt very carnal interest today in …"

Yet here we may helpfully return to the image of Jesus as healer and the comparison of this process of self-examination with the doctor's examination and diagnosis of a patient's condition. Certainly, an individual act such as one of those just mentioned is a sin in itself. But we may look below the surface, below the individual sinful act. Here we go away from straightforward moral theology into the realm of psychology, but this brief crossing of the border is necessary.

That individual act of pride may be the result of a settled habit, one that I have acquired because I have been recognized (or because I have not been recognised!) as being good at something. I come to look down on others. Here, it is not the individual act that needs to be perceived but the habit that gives rise to it.

But there may also be causes for my attitudes for which I have no responsibility. Prolonged and systematic abuse may instil an attitude of anger, so that I cannot love the abuser, and my behaviour towards others may be accounted for in the light of what has happened to me. In such cases there is the need to examine behaviour. A sudden flash of anger is one thing, but continued and regular anger should lead me to ask whether I want to behave in that way. Sin lies in accepting the behaviour, not in exhibiting it. If help can be had I should seek it.

What about the others?

If you read the story of the Exodus it is hard to avoid thinking that not all the Egyptian charioteers could have deserved to drown. The same might be said of others involved in wrong but whose sufferings seem disproportionate to their share or to the extent to which they might be held responsible.

First, of course, one must remember that obedience to orders is not always an excuse. That was the principle on which prosecutions for war crimes were based, and there is always the need to remember that no one ceases to be a human being.

Secondly, however, the sufferings of those Egyptian charioteers, as of the ordinary Nazi soldier and his family, were part of the sin of those in charge. So, for example, not only did Pharaoh sin against Israel, he sinned against his own people. This is one more case of human solidarity, and of how that solidarity is worked out in responsibility.

It is also one more case of how suffering should not always lead to the question *What have I done wrong?* When we see someone suffer we ought to ask whether our wrongdoing has contributed to that suffering. This is particularly important for Christians and the church because our attitudes may contribute to situations in which others suffer whilst we are secure in our sanctity.

All the virtues - except love

We have probably all met the kind of person who is very self-effacing, but by that attitude draws to herself/himself a lot of attention. Most of us have probably exercised patience to an incredible degree with someone, but it has been obvious that we were doing so. One's kindness may be remarked on by all in the family, but that very fact shows the potential use of that kindness as a lever for extracting acts of gratitude to reciprocate, and the other person could not possibly say 'No' after all one has done for him or her, a point often made implicitly if not explicitly.

In 1 Corinthians 13 Saint Paul warns about the danger of right things without love, whether what we should call the morally right things, such as giving one's goods to feed the poor, or the spiritually right things, like having faith. But in Colossians 3:12–17 a more basic list of virtues is given and Paul exhorts his audience to put on over the top love to hold everything in place. He depicts the virtues as garments ("Clothe yourselves") and love is here in the place of a belt, tied around to stop these virtues from sliding about and helping them to do what they are meant to do, just as a warm robe is no good if it is constantly falling off your shoulders or tripping you up.

Here, love is not one virtue among others; rather, it is the directing virtue, the rudder to make sure that all the other virtues do their work (if that is an appropriate way to speak of them) and the whole ship is heading in the right direction.

Question time again

Perhaps lists of questions for self-examination should include such items as these:
When did you last laugh? at what or whom?
When did you last laugh at yourself?
When did you last experience joy?
When did you last bring joy to another?
Are you suspicious of your pleasures? Why?
So how do you come through those questions?

We can find it difficult to focus, and sometimes there are particular things to which we find it especially hard to pay attention. Think of any of these things in your life. Tiredness can be a straightforward problem, or we may find it hard to pay attention to a particular speaker because of the manner of delivery. We can hardly be at fault for that. But we can reasonably ask ourselves, *What of the kingdom of God is there in that task or that speech?* That can or should hold our attention, and we may pray for grace to focus on what is important. Again, we may ask, *Why do other people think this is important?* And then we may attend for their sake, if not for our own.

On cynicism, we may ask how consistent we are in forming our judgements. *Am I particularly hard on a group or an individual? Am I always ready to believe the worst of them? Why?*

On keeping out of trouble, we may ask, *What things do I want to do, and what inhibits me from doing them?* If the answer to that is that I avoid doing something because it is wrong, I may ask, *Why it is deemed wrong?* Such a questioning may strengthen my moral stance by enabling me to grow or it may free me to do something, helping me grow in another way. Either way, I am a winner.

How well have I taken on board the basis of my morality? Do I avoid doing something more because of the shame detection would bring on me than because of the harm I might cause others? In itself that may be enough to stop me from doing a certain kind of harm, but there is still the need to look at what else is going on. I may feel instinctively that something is wrong, and perhaps I should go with that instinct because that may guard my mental balance. But such a way of forming a judgement or shaping actions is not adequate for commending a particular way of behaving to others, and so this may be a case of the need for tolerance of alternative judgements.

A look at the Bible

Sloth as lack of awareness and failure to question oneself when enjoying power is well portrayed in the description of the Egyptians as they held Israel in slavery and then were led to free their slaves given in Wisdom 17:20–21 and 18:14–19. (Though this is not in the Bible as Protestants read it, this book is background to much that shaped thinking at the time of Jesus.) What, in terms of wrong, do we take for granted? Do we accept something because things have always been that way and we are comfortable with the way things are?

Read Matthew 26:36–45. How do I keep watch with Christ?

The whole of Psalm 119 calls for slow, verse by verse meditation, but we may begin by having our attitude to law challenged and seeing it as gift, not burden. So think for a bit about Psalm 119:18, 105, 106. Such verses challenge both sloth and ignorance.

Forgetfulness is well illustrated in Psalm 106:6–15 and Hosea 11:1–9. But do I take what God has given for granted and fail to live a life that reflects gratitude?

Read Colossians 3:12–17. Notice how often thanksgiving is mentioned. This is one reason why it is a good reading for a wedding service. But gratitude is also being encouraged as a theme in our daily living.

Hosea also has a warning about superficial repentance. You can read Hosea 6:1–6 in two tones of voice: one expressing sincerity and perception of sin in verses 1–3, the other suggesting an attitude of 'Let's say "Sorry" again and it will be all right.' Part of the process of confession is resolution not to sin again. Is that in my mind when I say a prayer of confession in church? Forgetfulness and sloth are again stalking here.

5. Nothing Impersonal

Things so far may have seemed a bit heavy, so

I'll tell you a story.

In a large town in the Midlands, Mr. Rhyt-Price was arrested, charged and convicted of living off immoral earnings, that is, the proceeds of on-goings in the four large Edwardian houses he owned. He was duly remanded on bail before being sentenced. His story appeared in the local press and caused various reactions. At first, people were quick to dismiss him and his crime – sometimes with allusions to his ethnic background. But before he appeared in court for sentence, strange things happened.

The strange things began at the local Pentecostal Church. There are many in England who delight to call themselves Church of England. They do not go to church, they believe they do not need to, but they like church as a setting for family occasions. They claim to know what a church should be like and in their eyes it certainly should not be like the Pentecostal church. There were such snobs in the town and they thought it only right that problems should arise at the Pentecostal Church. Some even laughed, but their laughter was to be wiped away as they received their financial punishment. At the Pentecostal Church giving was taken seriously, and the relatively small congregation still generated a large income. People often knew who gave what, for there was no shame in giving a little nor pride in giving much; rather, there was rejoicing at the provision of the Lord. One day, Pastor Samuels noticed that the Sunday collection was seriously low. He checked with his elders and found that the great hole in the church's finances was caused by the loss of Charlene Louise's generous offerings. Charlene Louise gave large sums weekly and had provided for projects in the church, but now, it seemed, she was out of work. Pastor Samuels, for the first time, discovered what her work had been. Now, among her other accomplishments, Charlene Louise could play the organ. Pastor Samuels was especially proud of the organ, an instrument that had belonged to his father, Pastor Arphaxad Samuels. (Charlene Louise was able to fulfil this ministry because Mr. Rhyt-Price's establishments did not work on Sunday. This was one of the abiding fruits of the fact that Mr. Rhyt-Price's grandfather had been a lay preacher at the Independent Baptist Chapel back in Llandidribdibdobwels.) However, Pastor Samuels saw the only trace of a silver lining in the dark financial cloud in the fact that when Charlene Louise had given money for the restoration and improvement of the instrument he had managed to dissuade the elders from affixing a brass plate to the pipe-case with the words *Pastor Arphaxad Samuels' organ, enlarged and first played upon by Charlene Louise ... 18th. October 1998.*

Yet the Pentecostal Church was not the only church to feel the pinch. Mr. Khumunbai was a greatly respected member of the community, a Rotarian and, though a pillar of his temple, he was kindly disposed to all good works and philanthropic endeavours springing from whatever faith. There was not a charity appeal in the district, not a local Scout troop or pensioners' club that had not at some time benefited from the donation of a raffle prize from Mr. Khumunbai. A secret known only to him, Mrs. O'Murphy-O'Connell and God was the fact that the pot-plants, quite harmless geraniums, innocent chrysanthemums and others, sold in his corner shop were all provided by Mrs. O'Murphy-O'Connell, and the proceeds from their sale went to support the boys' club at the Church of Saints Alphonse, Alfege and Alfalfa. Now Mr. Khumunbai had quite a large number of customers who clearly did not live in the area. He assumed they were simply men stopping off on their way home from work to pick up presents for their wives or the odd bottle of wine to accompany a special dinner. Yet with the conviction of Mr. Rhyt-Price, the takings in the shop dropped dramatically, for six or seven customers per day each buying a bottle of spirits or a large box of chocolates could make quite a difference. And Mr. Khumunbai realized that these customers from outside the area were Mr. Rhyt-Price's customers, too. They were buying their "guilt gifts". And whereas the younger ones might buy wine, the older ones often bought plants to pretend to a level of boring steadiness they had just escaped. With the liquidation of Mr. Rhyt-Price's business, Mr. Khumunbai's takings fell by several hundred pounds a week, and included in the victims of this crash were Mrs. O'Murphy-O'Connell and the boys of Saints Alphonse, Alfege and Alfalfa.

Sniffily superior to all the local tradesmen's concerns was Miss Witherem, owner and headmistress of the local nursery. She read the newspaper story about Mr. Rhyt-Price with the right measures of disgust, contempt and curiosity, and then she turned to the business of running her nursery. *As well such places have been closed*, she thought. *My mothers ought not to be propositioned on their way to pick up their children.* But the ways of God striking the haughty are as wonderful as the ramifications of economics. Within a short time of Miss Witherem's disgust, children were being withdrawn from the nursery at an alarming rate. And because the children of Mr. Rhyt-Price's former employees were withdrawn when their mothers could no longer pay the fees, financial pressure meant that fees had to be raised for the children still attending. The abolition of a vicious practice led to a vicious spiral, as fewer and fewer parents could afford to send their children to Miss Witherem's establishment. Soon, another large Edwardian house was vacated as the nursery was forced to close. Miss Witherem left the area with sadness but with her pension intact. She had found a buyer for the large house that had been her nursery, such a nice man, a Mr. Gwd-Evans, who said in passing that his uncle owned some property in the area. She felt relieved that her school, as she still thought of it, was not going to a complete stranger. Nevertheless, she brooded on her life and livelihood in that town over the previous few years, though she could never subsequently bring herself to visit that part of town from sadness at what had been.

And not only among the younger section of the population was the damage to the social fabric felt. Mr. Rhyt-Price's employees had parents and grandparents, and for many of these grandparents it was the income from their grand-daughters that made the difference in where they could live, for the relative luxury of Coopem Hall Rest Home was more costly than the Council's provision in Scrimpit House. Again, economics bit, and not only residents of Coopem Hall who were related to Mr. Rhyt-Price's work-force had to move.

Such homes are used to a turn-over of residents, but the mass evacuation that came with the end of Mr. Rhyt-Price's business was comparable to a visitation of the Black

Death. No relief was available for the owners of Coopem Hall to carry them over in the short term until all places were filled again. And as the owners of Coopem Hall already had other financial commitments, the only thing they could do was serve notice on their residents. A solution to the plight of the residents was found when, once again, Mr. Gwd-Evans bought up the property. He realized that stimulation was very important for the elderly, and his coach trips to the Continent proved very popular with residents and other old people in the vicinity. How did he make ends meet? Perhaps you should ask Mr. Khumunbai, who was amazed (and relieved) to find an alternative and cheaper supplier of cigarettes. Then again, Mr. Khumunbai is quite innocent and probably would only be too glad to be a means of financing the care of older people to a standard everybody sees as desirable, and though not a smoker himself, he does not see the purchase of cigarettes as wrong. However, that is another story.

And what of Mr. Rhyt-Price? First, on the day of his appearance for sentencing, a number of respectable citizens gathered at the court, asking to serve as character witnesses. And their testimony amounted to: "We have all been living off immoral earnings." Secondly, Mr. Rhyt-Price was fined, but he had some help in paying the fine.

And where is he now? You can't keep an entrepreneur down. He is probably back in practice, perhaps in a town near you. Certainly, if he isn't, his nephew or son or brother will be, or his English cousin. (But Mr. Rhyt-Price prefers not to talk about *him*, for he does not observe the Sabbath respectfully.)

The story is a little laboured, but I hope you have enjoyed it. The only thing to bear in mind is the poet Horace's remark: "When the names are changed, it's of you that the tale is told."

Really?

So far, our look at self-examination has concentrated on what each of us can discover in ourselves as individuals. Although we know that, for many of the things that people do wrong, explanations can be found which reduce or even remove culpability, circumstances do alter cases. Despite the jokes which are often made about social workers or psychologists, we should not want the courts to return to the days when no account was taken of someone's background, the situation they were in or the conditions under which they had to live out their lives.

But if individual wrong-doers are to be understood before they are punished (so that the punishment can be proportionate to the responsibility of the offender), we need to remember that a circumstance common to all of us is the society in which we live and which has influenced us – and to which we have contributed and from which we have benefited. The harm and advantages are not evenly distributed, and there are those who genuinely have few of the things considered desirable by the society around them, whilst others seem to enjoy a superfluity of material goods and opportunities.

Now, there is such a thing as the politics of envy, a way of thinking which does not ask, "How are the less fortunate to be helped?" but, instead, is motivated by the premise that it must be wrong for someone to enjoy goods inaccessible to another. Such an approach demonises the wealthy and dehumanises them, ignoring the ways in which they may be victims and placing blame on individuals who are well-off while denying any culpability on the part of those who are not. Nevertheless, in the way goods are shared among the members of society, if those goods are the fruit of wrong, then those who share in them share in the wrong. Of course, even this claim can be modified. For example, the *guilt* of someone who steals on a grand scale from a poor country is undeniable, but it is possible to ascribe *blame* to the thief's descendants several generations later. This can be done so long as they are prepared to enjoy the fruits of the original wrong without regard for the disadvantage suffered by others which is a result of the perpetration of that wrong. That is, without directly committing the theft, they are in the position of receivers of stolen goods. All the same, the theft has created an imbalance, which has disadvantaged the poor and wrongly bestowed wealth on the thief, whose descendants share in the advantages of the theft. This imbalance will continue until what might be called *practical repentance* occurs; that is, the restitution or just sharing of the benefits that have accrued from the theft.

If this seems too idealistic, or even impractical, that appearance is merely an indicator of the scale of the problem. Like the characters in the story, we are the beneficiaries of the wrong done by others, and however much we may condemn that wrong we cannot separate ourselves from it.

But more than that, there is the simple fact that our lives are bound up with each other. What happens to one affects many, and the wrong or hurt that one person does or suffers affects those bound up in the network of human relationships. This network ultimately can link anyone with anyone, but we all know how it works through family, friends, colleagues and immediate neighbours. There was no such link, but physical proximity meant that the Samaritan was linked to the man who fell among thieves in the parable of the Good Samaritan at Luke 10:25–37, a link which the priest and the Levite denied by their actions. And when the priest and the Levite went on their way, perhaps to the services in the Temple, they took with them a kind of contamination. Imagine one of them saying to himself, *I must hurry, the congregation will be waiting and I must certainly avoid ritual pollution before taking part in the service.* The demand, real or imagined, placed on the leader of worship implicates the congregation in the wrong. They get their service at the expense of the man lying injured on the road.

Let us think about the story of Mr. Rhyt-Price again, for Miss Witherem, like most of us, is concerned about her pension. And look how she secures it! We can see the direct link between her money and Mr. Rhyt-Price's and Mr. Gwd-Evans' activities, whatever they might be. But our money is tied up in ways that make it no cleaner. And like Mr. Khumunbai, we derive benefit from activities which we should denounce. And like the residents of Coopem Hall, we benefit from the fact that somebody else is prepared to get their hands dirty.

Some words from the tradition

You may have a manual of devotion from your confirmation or some other aid to prayer and the Christian life. In some of these the following list appears:

Nine Ways of Participating in Another's Sin:

- by counsel
- by command
- by consent
- by provocation
- by praise or flattery

- by concealment
- by partaking (that is, sharing in the profit)
- by silence
- by defence of the ill done

Awareness of this inter-connectedness of sin is nothing new!

All in the same boat

It looks as though there is no way out of this situation. It is not just cynicism that makes us sceptical about revolutions, but the fact that revolutionaries are human and so liable to the limits, ignorance and temptations to which all flesh is heir. And even great leaders can provide only partial answers.

The recognition of this situation is nothing new. From before Christ, drama dealt with the theme of inherited guilt and responsibility. In the three plays known as the *Oresteia* by the Greek playwright Aeschylus (525–456 B.C.), a story is told of the urge for revenge and the quest for justice which involves members of a family in the murder of one another. The plight of a woman in the first play, who seeks redress for the slaying of her daughter, is balanced by the plight of her son in the second play, who has to avenge his father's murder. All of the characters could say that they are born into a world that has gone wrong.

On a grander scale, part of the case for Marxism lay in the recognition that individuals belong to groups, classes, and the individual's place in the world and access to its goods is in large measure determined by the class to which s/he belongs. One does not need to be a Marxist to see the force of this point.

In later drama, one of the best exposition of what Christians have called the doctrine of original sin is in one of Ibsen's plays, *Ghosts*. In this play, a mother (Mrs. Alving) and her adult son suffer the consequences of the late Captain Alving's wrongdoing. Mrs. Alving realizes that she has been held by her society and upbringing in a situation that has harmed others and herself.[1]

This is not an exclusively Western anxiety. In a very different religious setting, the problem is expounded and a solution hinted at in a short play called *Atsumori*, written in the fourteenth or fifteenth century in Japan. The play deals with the theme of reconciliation after civil war by pointing to the need for help from outside the situation. At the end of the play, Atsumori, the re-incarnation of a soldier slain by Rensei, has the chance to kill Rensei. The Chorus speaks these concluding words:

> "There is my enemy," he cries, and would strike,
> But the other is grown gentle
> And calling on Buddha's name
> Has obtained salvation for his foe;
> So that they shall be re-born together
> On one lotus-seat.
> "No, Rensei is not my enemy.
> Pray for me again, oh pray for me again."

Earlier, the Chorus speaks about Buddha thus:

> He bids the flowers of Spring
> Mount the tree-top that men may raise their eyes
> And walk on upward paths;
> He bids the moon in Autumn waves be drowned
> In token that he visits laggard men
> And leads them out from valleys of despair.[2]

Self-examination leads to examination of the self in its relationships and all that may be-foul us from those and all that we may contribute to the pain of others through them. We live through our relationships, and the practices of attack and defence impinge in ways we find hard to discern and painful to bear. "The burden of them is intolerable," as the General Confession of the Church of England's Book of Common Prayer says. We can be left with an end-of-term report which simply says, "Must try harder," or we can give up and live lives of superficiality in which we avoid all relationships of any depth or we can despair or go mad – or we can look for One Who visits laggard men and leads them out from valleys of despair. The despair seems to increase the more we strive for good because we become increasingly aware of how far short we fall. There is no final commentary on Saint Paul's Letter to the Romans, but two verses deserve to be pondered in this context:

> What a wretched man I am! Who will rescue me from this body of death? Thanks be to God – through Jesus Christ Our Lord! (Romans 7:24-25)

Perhaps the commentary on these words is to be found not in a book but in the lives of all who have confronted sin – their own and the world's – and been brought to see that they cannot and need not face it alone and that the world itself is not alone.

Question time, yet again

Are there situations in my life or the life of the world for which I am afraid to pray?

Are there people for whom I do not think it is appropriate to pray?

What does my intercession amount to for the American president,

> a tyrant who regularly figures in the news,
> an anti-Western terrorist,
> an extremist political party,
> an Islamist preacher,
> the models in pornographic magazines,
> a criminal who is an icon of evil,
> the Jehovah's Witnesses who last visited me,
> people who misuse churchyards,
> baptism families who seem not to be interested?

How far do I use my imagination in praying for such people?

Do I joke about sin or sins?

Do I pray for specific things for people, or do I sometimes simply hold the people before God?

Am I honest with God about my own confusion?

Do I see giving to Christian Aid (a U.K. based international charity) or some similar organisation as an act of charity or an act for justice?
Am I prepared to say, "Charity begins at home," – but let Jesus define *home*?

How much does the prayer "Lead us not into temptation" safeguard me or my church from risks?

How far does awareness of my own sin shape my attitude to the sin of others?
Does it make me humble?
Sympathetic?
Defensive?

How aware am I of the failings of groups of any sort to which I belong?
What am I doing about these failings?

Some work on the Bible

Read Psalm 25.
The psalm seems to be about an individual's situation, yet the last verse shifts attention to Israel.
Do I agonize with others in my praying?
Do I see my problems as problems of the groups to which I belong?
Do I see the resolution of my problems in the resolution of problems in the groups to which I belong?
Do I use the resolution of my problems to benefit the groups to which I belong?

Read Nehemiah 5.
The people of Judah have been in exile and are now returning to Jerusalem and the surrounding area. They are trying to pick up the threads of life back in their homeland. Obviously, there are disparities of wealth.
Do I see my money as a trust from God?
Do I honour the people who make my wealth possible?
Do I bother about why some people are disadvantaged, or do I just accept it as the way the world is?

Read Matthew 13:31–32.

The kingdom of God is not the church (!) and it is obviously meant to be something in God's control, but He means us to share in its life and to be encouraged by it.

Do I despise small deeds of justice or mercy?

Do I despair of God's achieving His purpose? Why?

Do I blame myself for things beyond my control and so evade blame for things for which I am responsible?

Do I dwell on blaming myself, or do I hand the mess over to God in faith? Am I afraid to do so because I know what the answer might be?

Read Matthew 13:33.

Identifying the flour can be difficult! The individual and the group can at one time be the flour and at another time embody the yeast.

How do I let God's kingdom, His power and authority, work in my own life?

How do I let it work through me in the life of the church? or of the world?

The yeast blends with the flour.

Are there things I want to point to and say, "*I* did that"?

Am I jealous of the status of the church?

A concluding moral saying

If life is a rat-race, even if you win, you are still a rat.

6. We Are not Alone

The need to die

Many people these days seem to live easily with the view that after physical death there is nothing. Of course, much of the frantic quest for short-term satisfactions can be for some just a form of denial. Also, the belief that one ceases to be accountable at death is re-assuring for those who are aware of their failings. This is not talking about the egregious sinners, it is about those who see it as praiseworthy that they have "loved their homes," which is a way of saying that they have made themselves as comfortable as possible. It is about those who have denied shared humanity. It is about those who "would never stop anyone from going to church" but who have not seen the need of it themselves and expect God to be there as an insurance policy regardless. It is about those who have lived as though there were no god but expect Him to welcome them with open arms in the end. It is about those who have never committed great sins simply because of lack of imagination or through pusillanimity. And it is about those who have enjoyed going to church – even bemoaned the fact that others do not – but who have made not a move to encourage or welcome others, because they have come to church for a "religious fix" on their terms, not the transforming judgement and acquittal that come from Jesus, and so have made church a matter of taste, not of life.

For all these people, the visible and the immediate count, and death is the point of severance from the visible and the immediate, from all they have struggled to understand and, by understanding, to control.

It may be that such people die before they die. At Joe Bloggs's funeral, we are witnessing merely the tidying up of a physical thing, as Joe Bloggs, the child created by and for God, died years ago in a morass of selfishness and his body leaves the world to the accompaniment of the national anthem of hell, 'My Way'. Just as a limb can wither, so can a soul. But a withered limb is still connected to a body, and a withered soul can survive in suspended animation. Individuals, churches, groups and relationships can go into such states, like trees which have grown old and died from the inside. If you do not raise your eyes you never see the world.

Sin brings with it the drive to avoid dying in life, which is different from physical death. This is the meaning of both the headings under which we have looked at sin. Attack is about finding life by assertion and defence is about clinging to something we are afraid to let go in order to allow it to grow or to take its proper place in the past. People who have satisfied themselves that there is nothing after physical death (or who live as though there is not) are more keen than ever to evade the deaths we all must go through if we are to be free.

Death stands for the end of all attacking because it is impervious to attack. Sooner or later it will happen, and though it may lose battles, the war, it seems, it will always win. And death makes a mockery of all defensiveness. (For those who enjoy cinema – if *enjoy* is the right word in this case – the treatment of death in Ingmar Bergmann's *The Seventh Seal* is hard to beat as an illustration of all this.) And yet both attacking and defending lead to death because the urge constantly to be on the attack means the elimination of everybody else. And the quest for the perfect defensive position means the denial of access to all that might nourish the person.

Few people go all the way with one or the other, and those who seem to are often viewed as suffering from psychiatric illness. But this has more to do with our own inconsistency than with innate virtue. However, where love is experienced there is a break in the system of defence or the urge to attack – and love is a work of divine subversion in the fortress of sin. We can be cheered by the thought that Jesus was a subversive, and the most subversive thing He did was to die. By His dying He upsets all the norms and things we take for granted. God loved the world so much that He turned His back on all the false ways it has of defending or expressing itself. On the cross, Jesus says, "I don't need *and you don't need* all those things you think go to make you so secure or powerful." There is much in the Letter to the Colossians that you can think you have grasped but then it comes to you in a different light, and there is much that is based on allusion rather than direct reference. Perhaps this view of Christ as the subversive could help us understand the treatment of the Crucifixion, the subversive's death *par excellence*, in Colossians 2:13–15.

Often in Christian thinking death has been viewed only as the wages of sin. Yet there is much in each of us which would be better cauterised, killed. From the death that is the wage of sin we can be delivered by the acceptance that we can welcome the death of certain things which are not really ourselves in the first place. Over the course of years, someone who has suffered, say, a leg injury, can walk with a limp. It seems to be part of them; they do not notice it, and everybody knows what is the matter and what sort of allowances to make. And yet that limp is not part of the person. So with a settled habit of sin, we can accept its death because it is not part of us. This does not mean that the process will not be painful. Imagine someone who has come to accept that they never talk to some other person. This habit becomes fixed and goes on until, perhaps, even the original reason for the breach is forgotten. That does not matter because views will be slanted and there will be a built-in readiness to think ill of the other or to mock them or to look down on them or just to ignore him or her. For this to end, to die, a recognition of its wrongfulness, the fact that it is out of place is required. This may mean that one must see how ridiculous or proud or hurtful one has been. It may require a readiness to accept a hurt from the past, for the one seeking reconciliation may have been in the right, but the healing is important. The death will be painful, but it is necessary. If another picture may be used, we can imagine a boat which has acquired loads of barnacles. The barnacles are not part of the boat, and all they do is stop the boat from gliding smoothly through the water. Scraping the barnacles off is necessary, but the process may scratch the hull of the boat.

A second kind of death is also needed, and it is related to this death of sin. In fact, it is the death of false images of oneself. Sometimes we have an image of what we are to become, sometimes an image of how we hope others see us now. Sometimes it is an image of ourselves that enables us to live with ourselves – we portray ourselves as victims or saints or always needed or wiser than the rest (sometimes as so wise we should only be misunderstood if we spoke!) or patient (so patient we make others ache with our patience) or generous (to the point of flooding the world in our seeking to control or buy) or forgiving (in a way which is exemplary – and an example is wasted if it is not seen). But the image of what we are to become can be as harmful because it sets false goals or breeds dissatisfaction. We might think, *I'll be happy when I accomplish this goal,* and that often leads to *I'll be happy* only *when I accomplish this goal.* Envy or greed can spring from this assertiveness. Others are made unhappy in minor ways or major ways as the quest for my fulfilment takes over. And that fulfilment can be sought in many ways. The gross materialistic fulfilments are the least of our worries. Most people are helped to overcome these in childhood when they confront the facts of limited pocket money and unlimited toy-shops! But the wish to be "very spiritual" can lead to all sorts of rubbish, harmful to the person and to those with whom s/he comes into contact. The image of oneself as the best prime minister the country never had can lead to laughter in the pub, but if it goes "underground" and the frustrated wish for power is not dampened, there can be havoc in the home.

Again, this death can be painful. It demands that we accept ourselves as ordinary and must learn to rejoice in the ordinary. Yet how much calmer such a life can be! *Ordinary* does not mean *boring* or *unimportant* or *second-rate* or *dull.* The world of nature is full of the ordinary, yet it fascinates the observer and its very ordinariness is a condition of the thriving of individuals and species. There is something profoundly sad about the couple who divorce within six months because of boredom. Indeed, a good relationship needs the ordinary. To be ordinary demands balance. An eccentric genius can justify (at least to herself/himself) all kinds of behaviour we should normally think of as anti-social. The pursuit of extraordinary virtue is often associated with those who live as monks or nuns, but the pursuit of ordinariness as a virtue is how the fabric of the community is maintained. Those held up to us as heroes need the anonymous punctuality of 'bus drivers and bakers, the post office delivering in all kinds of weather, and the mending of roads on which they can travel to preach to thousands or perform their deeds of charity. Even the production of Lent study notes or a book on self-examination brings temptation!

Yet there is a further death, and this must be the hardest of all. It is not the death of something external to our real selves; it is the death of self. Even that which is good is to be handed over to God to be grown. If the grain does not die it remains a single grain, but if it dies ... See John 12:20–33. This was the pattern of Jesus' living and dying, and though ours are qualitatively different, still we are called upon to take up the cross appointed for us, to die to self, to be crucified with Christ. Such a dying is the denial of both the felt need to attack and the desire to defend. It is not denying the value of the life that has been given – and lived – but the acceptance that its fulfilment is in something not to be measured from within its own limits. Job's cry – "Yea, though He slay me, yet is He God" – is fulfilled in the cry from the cross: "It is perfected." I can see the point of slaying the nasty bits in me, even if I don't like it at the time. But the good bits? Must they go too?

First, they need to be held as not the whole person. The good which has been done and the good qualities one may have gained are like voices urging one on: "You have done that, so you can do this." In this sense, we have to be on guard against making the really good things in our lives idols. In this way, we must be ready to lose the good things of the past. Heaven may be shaped by gratitude, but surely it will not be just about looking back through a photograph album.

But secondly, and as a blow to that pride which is the fundamental sin, we must recognize that, as God made us, we are valued and so, just as God will deal with the bad bits, He will look for *us*, for whole people, not a few fragments of good. God is concerned with the whole person, not those bits we shouldn't mind others seeing. We must be prepared to leave the good we have done or become behind and, turning to be like children, learn to accept from God and go on accepting. Many people have heard the words: "The wages of sin is death." Often, these words are often used as an excuse for exulting over the misfortune of someone reckoned publicly to be a sinner. Yet how much better if people remembered the words which follow: "But the gift of God is eternal life in Christ Jesus Our Lord" (Romans 6:23).

Our self-examination can help us be grateful for the good, but it can also help if we look for similar good in others. Thus, we can begin to receive in the way in which we received as children, that is, through other people. And then, without denying the reality of that good, we can think how much greater is the good that comes from God. Does somebody else show gentleness in dealing with us in a particular situation? Jesus says, "I am meek and you will find rest for your souls." Does someone else show patience? Jesus longs to gather us to Himself as a hen gathers her brood, and He works healings even when confronted with a faithless generation. Does somebody else offer practical help? What is more practical than feeding crowds? Does someone else forgive? Hear the faultless One say, "Does no one condemn you? Neither do I," and we can cut through our self-recrimination, and even more, from our cross itself, say "Father, forgive them."

As we reflect in this way, we can go beyond thinking of what another person has done as being good (but Grade *B* good, whereas what God does is Grade *A* good). We can see the good done by other people as expressing God's goodness and so be led to gratitude to God and for the good and for the other person.

From the good we see in others we are led to picture the greater good and then, through seeing it reflected in others, we are enabled to think we can do it. But then we can afford also to say that the good is a matter of response. I do good because I have received it; I do not do good in order to earn it.

You died

Such are the words of Saint Paul in writing to the Christians in the town of Colossae. And he goes on to write, "And your life is now hidden with Christ in God." And when did this dying occur?

The imagery of baptism as dying is found in Saint Paul, and it is worthwhile to be technical for a moment. The Greek tense Paul uses when he says, "You died" is one that implies a single event in the past. It might be possible to link that statement to the death of Adam, but this would make nonsense of the setting. *You died* at one event, and now you are bound up in Christ. The only event which could make sense of the combination of these two ideas – dying and being hidden in Christ – is baptism, a single, once-for-all event. Yet the baptism gets its meaning from the Death of Jesus. *You died* when Jesus did, your dying was already there in the love of God. Perhaps we should see the death as not happening in baptism but as being realized in it.

Familiarity breeds contempt, and we are too familiar with baptism – in one way. Yet we cannot be too familiar with it. Think of the background: Jesus died and rose from death. The human race as a whole and individual human beings are all caught up in the round of sin and death. But people are afforded the way out of that round by being joined to Jesus in His dying and rising. In the course of sin, we are influenced by – belong to – all manner of things. Our being joined to Jesus means a new belonging, or, rather, the recovery of the belonging that was there at creation but from which we have been drawn away. And the means by which we are joined to Jesus is baptism.

In the early church the rites of baptism were described as "hair-raising"! The candidates, usually adults, had undergone a long period of preparation. On the evening before Easter Sunday they gathered outside the church. They renounced evil (even physically turning from facing West to facing East, in expectation of the rising Sun, standing for light, and of the Resurrection of Jesus). And then, after readings and prayers, they were baptized *by total immersion*, symbolising the dying, burial, and rising of Jesus. Further ceremonies followed, including signing with the cross, the mark of the army in which and the commander under Whom the Christian was to serve. And then the newly baptized were given an oil lamp, not just to find their way in the darkness outside the church but also to signify the fact that they had received the light of Jesus and were called to shed that light in their lives. And then they walked in procession into the church where they were welcomed by the congregation and they received a drink of milk with honey in it, which symbolized their entry into the Promised Land. The service continued with the Eucharist, and the newly-baptized did not just receive communion for the first time then; indeed, this was the first time they had attended the full Communion service.

How does our approach to baptism – our own baptism – compare with that? Discipline was strict in the early church, so Christians lived up to the renunciation they had made. If, as Christians, we are called to die daily, then we are meant to live out lives of renunciation of evil. This sounds negative, but if we think in terms of turning, then we are encouraged to turn to that which is light and live.

Do we live as though dead to sin? Now if you are dead as far as something is concerned, that something is dead as far as you are concerned. Therefore, for the Christian sin is a dead thing. This means that we need not fear it. We avoid it out of love for God, but by concentrating on the love of God, we can be delivered from even thinking of it. This is a high ideal because the fascination with sin can draw us in, but the Christian life is not about the avoidance of vice but growth in love. (This is where the constant use of the prayer 'O God, make speed to save me; O Lord, make haste to help me' or a readines to use it when aware of temptation can help.)

And do we dwell on the dead things of the past? We may reflect on them, but we need to recover that sense of the Easter baptismal services of looking back to the Exodus, a story that is still central in the Easter Vigil service. We celebrate the fact of deliverance rather than being fascinated (and so still held captive by) the power of evil.

And do we look to the future with the hope that the Resurrection breathes?

Again, we may compare baptism with a wedding. The newly baptized were marked with the cross in recognition of new obligations and tasks. Baptism brings these as it also brings the promise of help in fulfilling these responsibilities. In that sense it is like a wedding. The partners each know they are taking on a commitment accepting new obligations. But they do this in response to the gift of a partner, and they receive help in the fulfilment of these obligations from the very one to whom they are obligated. So the signing with the cross is both the acceptance of a burden and the recognition that one cannot carry that burden on one's own (nor is one expected to do so).

The light given at baptism is one to which we can turn still. When suffering his darkest depressions and feeling most alienated from God, Martin Luther could shout confidently, "I have been baptized!" and in this receive strength. To know that, before we could do a thing to help ourselves, God reached out for us in Jesus and took us to Himself in Jesus through the objective fact of our baptism is something we can take for granted as a means of growth. But we dare not take it for granted when it comes to presuming on God's love. However, if we may continue the wedding imagery, there is no such thing as a private marriage, however personal each marriage must be. The fact of marriage has an impact on others, and our being joined to God must do the same. Living up to our baptism cannot but help others, and living in a way that denies our baptism will push others further from God. "By their fruits you shall know them" is an unavoidable test.

In the new baptism service in the Church of England no attempt has been made to use the ceremony of giving a drink of milk and honey. (Perhaps we should be grateful for small mercies, but even now there is probably a sub-committee of the Liturgical Commission exploring ways of incorporating this.) Yet we can ask whether our lives are lived in the light of what God has done. This is symbolized by but not confined to the deliverance from Egypt and the gift of the land. And do we live in the light of what God has promised (the fulfilment of all that the gift of the land stood for in the experience of Israel and in its subsequent understanding of what it meant to be the people of God)? In our self-examination, do we look for things for which to give thanks? And do we ask ourselves what it would mean for God to fulfil His promises in our lives, individually or as a church or as a race? Do we believe, as the Old Testament prophets taught, that God's purpose for us is good? And do we believe, as the prophets taught, that that purpose is for a people, not for individuals?

Much of this might seem to go a long way away from the traditional treatment of self-examination, but it is the foundation and framework of Christian self-examination. The recovery of the true self is the goal of that process, and the self can only be understood in relation to its dependences and its direction. Self-examination without reference to God will be misleading and destructive; with reference to God it will be purifying (and so, at times, painful), but it will also be a way by which we are put back in touch with the source of life and the God-given means of feeding life – that is, among other things, our human relationships.

All together now

Much has been said about belonging and about the different parts of our individual lives. We are shaped by our relationships and the creation of the church through the honest use of baptism is God's way of shaping a new way of relating. This is why, in some methods of self-examination questions of one's relationship(s) with the church form a separate section, for those who worship with one, brothers and sisters by baptism, are not just any other neighbours. Several times in the letters in the New Testament, love within the church is mentioned as something distinct from love of one's neighbour. The church has been described as a school of love. By God's gift, we have been brought into relationship within the church, just as two people are God's gift to each other in marriage. But that does not mean that the relationship within the church is not to be worked at any less than the relationship within marriage. God's grace is not a substitute for human love, but rather, it is the inspiration for it, and it enables us to grow in the image of God, Who is not a robot and has not made us to be robots.

What now?

When was the last time I gave thanks for someone in the congregation?
What about for someone at work?
What about for someone who helps in daily life?
What about for a member of my family?
How did I express my gratitude to God?
How did I express it to the person concerned?

What events or experiences in my life could I interpret in terms of Exodus or the entry into the Promised Land?
Do I expect life as a Christian to be easy?
What makes it difficult?
Who or what makes these difficulties?

Do I find joy in receiving Holy Communion?

If somebody says to me, "I'm a Christian. Are you?" does that start alarm bells ringing?

Are there aspects of myself that I think God does not like?
Are they aspects that I do not like?
Do I find pleasure in them?
So can I cope with ambiguous feelings about myself?

And can I trust God to accept me in my muddledness and confusion?

Are there people I hold back in any way?
Do I make myself the focus of attention?
Do I measure others' feelings, circumstances, pains or experiences by my own?
Which is more important to me: that I succeed or that the task in which I am involved succeeds?

If I had to choose a few pages from the Bible to take on my desert island, which would they be? Why? Re-read those words and give thanks for those pages.

Some work on the Bible

Read Colossians 1:1–6.

The words "We have heard of your faith in Christ Jesus and of the love you have for all the saints" (N.I.V.) can sound narrow, as though what matters is only love within the church. But we can place the emphasis in two places:

either

"We have heard of … the love you have for all the *saints*"

or

"We have heard of … the love you have for *all* the saints."

Think about that difference.

Are there people within the church of whom I think, *What are they doing here?*

If someone knew me as I know me, might they be forgiven for thinking the same?

What makes the difference between the fellowship or love to be found in any club and the love to be expected in a Christian congregation?

Read 1 John 3:6.
This verse seems to call into question anyone's claim to be a Christian if they are not perfect! We know that we fail regularly and often go back to the same sins. However, we might draw a comparison with other ways of describing expectations. For example, "A pupil of this school would not ..." is the headmaster's way of telling pupils off for doing just that thing! "A real craftsman would ..." expresses a standard to which to aspire, though craftsmen may differ. "If you practise, you will be able to ..." recognizes shortcoming, but it also acknowledges the attainability of the goal.
Do I see living the Christian life as a matter of acquiring a set of rules on which to draw or as a matter of acquiring sensitivity to myself, others and God?
Am I too easily satisfied?
What makes me dissatisfied with my life? Is that realistic?

So, read 1 John 1:8–10 and 2:1.
Jesus is our advocate with the Father, the guarantee that we shall be heard by love. Yet Jesus cannot be our *advocate* with ourselves. We need to accept that our judgement of ourselves is faulty and shift our attention from our condemnation of ourselves to God's diagnosis.

Read John 5:1–7.
Do I give reasons why I cannot receive God's healing?

Have I become used to being only half-alive in certain areas of my life?

Is it easier for me to stay paralysed than to face what comes with the ability to walk?

Some ancient words of encouragement

As a handful of sand thrown into the ocean, so are the sins of all flesh as compared with the mind of God.

Just as a strongly flowing fountain is not blocked up by a handful of earth, so the compassion of the Creator is not overcome by the wickedness of His creatures.[1]

7. Here We Don't Go Again

Excellence comes as standard

Everybody seems to know how to use the word *good*, but it is among the most slippery eels in the sea of language. Often it is used as a word of commendation. This use begins at school – from a tick to the writing of "Good" at the end of a piece of work, a teacher might encourage pupils to look forward to the even higher accolade of "Very Good" and perhaps from there the dizzying heights of "Excellent" (perhaps with a star!) could be glimpsed. In later life, someone may be spoken of with the word *good* when a neighbour is wishing to speak highly of him or her. "He is good. He visits his parents every week, even though he lives so far away," for example, or, "She is good; she shops for old Mrs. Ramsbottom, even though they are not related." Somehow, these people are considered out of the ordinary. It is assumed that you would have no reason for expecting this kind of behaviour from any normal human being.

It is hard but it has to be said that this is not a Christian view. There is another use of the word *good* which commends in a different way. There can be good examples of something. Hitler was a good example of a tyrant. But more subtly than that, we can see that a good example of, a good specimen of the human race would be one in which the qualities we think most important in being human are to be seen. To say of someone "He is a good violinist" is to pick something at which he excels. To say "He is a good man" implies that he excels at being – human. He is a good specimen. But the comparison breaks down because being human is not an optional activity for human beings, nor is it a competitive activity. In this case, being good is not something that leads to commendation, though not being good may be reason for condemnation. Also, we are judged by our choice of criteria for applying the word *good*. In talking in this way, I am not riding a hobby-horse. Back in the Middle Ages, one great theologian distinguished uses of *good* by pointing out that a sample of urine could be called a good sample even if it indicated poor health.

And this seems to be the implication of some words in the Gospel according to Saint Luke (17:7–10). Why should God not expect the best of us? And how can we think in terms of putting God in our debt, which is the implication of the first use of *good* (the "Look-at-all-I've-done-for-you" approach)? Do you remember Saint Mark the Ascetic? He has some words on this topic:

> Wishing to show that to fulfil every commandment is a duty, whereas sonship is a gift given to men through His own Blood, the Lord said: 'When you have done all that is commanded you, say: 'We are useless servants: we have only done what was our duty' (Luke 17:10). Thus the kingdom of heaven is not a reward for works, but a gift of grace prepared by the Master for His faithful servants.

Further on, the same writer warns against a credit-and-debit approach to our relationship with God. He writes:

> If we are under an obligation to perform daily all the good actions of which our nature is capable, what do we have left over to give to God in repayment for our past sins?[1]

But take heart

Jesus was asked by Peter how often he should forgive his brother. Peter suggested seven times, but Jesus replied, "Not seven times, but seventy times seven," and He went on to tell the story of the unmerciful servant (Matthew 18:21–35). Though that parable may be meant to show our duty of forgiveness, the picture it gives of God is worth considering. Yes, He is the one who condemns the unmerciful, the one Who allows them to live in the universe as fashioned by their laws. But what if we think again of Peter's question? He is not asking, "What size of sin should I forgive?"; he is asking, "How often should I forgive?" What if someone keeps on doing something which will not cause me real harm but makes it seem as though they are unaware of what they are doing? Can sins be banked? Do one thousand thoughtless speeches add up to one serious injury? And just because I put up with someone who was a pain yesterday, do I have to put up with him or her to-day?

And the answer in Jesus' parable is both uncomfortable and comforting. It is uncomfortable because it is a straight: "Yes, you must put up with him." It is comforting because it implies that God has that kind of patience with us. If God expects not just one-off grand acts of forgiveness of us but daily acts of 'little forgivenesses', can we not look for the same extensive as well as intensive forgiveness? It is pride which makes one say, "This sin is too big for God to forgive," but it is also pride to say, "I have exhausted God's forgiveness."

Those who take up this thought and say, "Well, in that case it doesn't matter what I do. God will forgive me all the time," have missed the point. They are playing at relating to God. A man who said, "My wife loves me so much that it doesn't matter if I hurt her," has missed the point. The fact of his wife's love should make him all the more keen not to hurt her. In the same way one can think, *God loves me so much that it doesn't matter if I crucify Him again with my sinning*. That position ignores the meaning of that love. Rather, the Christian should think, *God loves me so much that I will try not to hurt Him*. Often, something like this is heard when people talk about sacramental confession. They think that people go to confession only to go out and commit the same sins again without regard for what they have just said. Sometimes an insulting caricature of Roman Catholics is thrown in for good measure! Of course, purpose of amendment, the intention within the penitent's mind not to sin again, is fundamental to making a real confession, but we continue to live in a world of temptations. Remember: going to the gym once or twice will not turn anybody into an Olympic athlete!

So why does the world seem the same?

Those who take Christianity as just morality with a few stories added are doomed to frustration and disappointment, for Christian morality is quite different from other moralities in its list of demands – it is as much a commandment of Christ to receive Communion as to love our neighbour – and in its view of humanity – we are not independent, autonomous moral agents capable of making up our own minds from a kind of intellectual or spiritual high ground. Most importantly, Christians speak of something called *grace,* which is meant to enable them to do good. Some talk of 'living in the Spirit' as though God were in control of their lives, not just as one giving instructions, but as one giving the power to carry out those instructions.

Yet it has to be said (to put it mildly) that living the Christian life does not seem easy. And the failings and failures of Christians look very much like those of their non-Christian friends.

First, we are back to the talk of specimens. There are times when the action in question (not the person) is a good example of a Christian action. God is creating us, by His commandments, but He is not working with inanimate matter. His will is to create loving beings, not robots. Therefore, at times, the material will be recalcitrant, the clay will answer back to the potter. Yet even the failures and failings can be used by the Craftsman in the shaping of the finished product. By knowing some of my sins I can learn sympathy and can be led to praise God Whose love holds on to me. In the Middle Ages such an approach as this was used by some to answer the question: "Why did God let Adam and Eve sin?" The answer was what is known as the *felix culpa* explanation. (The Latin words mean *happy fault.*) The sin of Adam and Eve gave scope for God to reveal His love in ways in which it could not otherwise be known. At first this seems odd, but we may think of the *culpa* (the sin) as being turned so as to give a happy outcome. God does not re-write the past; He heals it and uses it.

Secondly, love is about the building up of a relationship. There is all the difference in the world between the wedding and the marriage, yet nothing can destroy the fact of the wedding. A married couple are building the boat on which they are sailing after it has been launched. So for the Christian, our lives are not just collections of deeds good or bad; rather, they are about living in a set of relationships in which we are led to know God and ourselves.

But thirdly, the Christian life, like any form of human life, is not lived in isolation. As Christians, we are meant to be amphibious creatures. We learn more and more about the way animals make an impact on their environment. What a creature picks up on the land it carries into the water and vice versa.

We live in the kingdom of God – our citizenship is in heaven – but we also live – and must live – in a world which has gone wrong. Yet we must depend upon this world. This world was created by God. There is a great difference between believing that the world has gone wrong and believing that it is thoroughly evil and we must flee from it. God so loved the world that He gave His only Son, remember. So long as there is in the world anything out of harmony with the ways of God, so long will we all be liable to sin, for we cannot know how or when or where that which is wrong will have an impact on our own lives, and we are called to work to remedy that wrong. Our being so bound up together is one reason why we should not despair at our failings, but neither should we blame others for them.

But also we carry things between these two realms. We need the world of work and entertainment, of political activity and art, of social life and the countryside and all those other things that make up what many think of as normal human life – we need them as much as anybody. Yet that does not mean the world in which we encounter them is perfect. But the other world, the other part of our environment as amphibians, is not the church. That is embedded in the world. (Of course, there are sects which claim that their church is the kingdom and draw a strict line between what happens in church and among members of the sect and what happens elsewhere. It is possible without cynicism at such a naive approach still to see in it a reproduction of the worst aspects of Pharisaism.)

The complementary part of our environment, the other half of a complete world we need to flourish as human beings, is defined by neither a place nor an activity. Instead, it is defined by a relationship, our relationship with God. The words *the kingdom of God*, which are often found in the New Testament, do not refer to an island floating somewhere, a place to which we are to come. The word *kingdom* might better be translated as *kingship*. When Jesus says "The kingdom of God is like ..." He is not describing a place; rather, He is saying, "This is how God exercises His kingship, this is what it means to call God *King*." If Jesus can be seen as a subversive, overturning the standards and expectations of the world around Him, He can also be seen as the perfect amphibian. Indeed, He is able to live in both parts of His environment and enrich both parts by what He brings from one to the other. Now we can be most "worldly" in our activities in church, and a church meeting can be as sour and acrimonious as any other meeting. Yet as individuals and as the church which claims to be the body of Christ for a place we are called to bring from our relationship with God that which makes of the affairs of the world expressions of His kingdom, in love and beauty, creativity and healing, justice and peace. We have learnt of God through imperfect human beings, and we, imperfect as we are, seek to pass on the knowledge of God. Our lives and words are thus mixtures of the divine, the kingdom of God expressed through us, and the human, the fallen and spoilt. We are saved and we are in the process of being saved, for all our relationships are to be set right, the good ones and the bad. It should be no surprise that very often we find it hard to discern what in any situation is of God and what is not. We are not in the position of Adam, before the fall, nor of the restored humanity in heaven. We are in between. And it is because we have come into the story part way through that we have problems.

As was said, we are shaped by our relationships, and the background of those relationships is in a world that has been marred by generations of attacking and defending. And it is into the renewing of our relationship with God that we enter at baptism, and through that renewed relationship we can become what we are meant to be. But this does not remove us from part of an environment that is wrong and continues to influence us. One of the best ways of describing the situation can be found in some words of Gregory of Nyssa (335–c.394). He writes in answer to someone who raises the problem of sin after Jesus has died for us, overcoming evil, and we have been joined to Him in baptism:

> If anyone thinks to refute our argument on the ground that even after the application of the remedy man's life is still discordant through his errors, let us guide him to the truth by an illustration from familiar experience. Take the case of a snake: it may receive a fatal blow on the head, but the coil behind is not immediately deprived of life along with the head; the head has died, but the tail part is kept alive by its own spirit, and is not deprived of its vital motion. Similarly, we can see wickedness fatally smitten, but still troubling the life of man in its remnants.[2]

This might seem pessimistic: you go through the whole process of baptism and striving to live the Christian life, and yet you seem still to be trapped and tripped by the snake. Yet we are also taken back to the image of death. It is the snake that has died; sin and death are dead things.

Healing analogies have been used frequently, and one more is in place here. After a successful operation to mend a leg there can still be the need for a time of recovery. Muscles must grow again and the patient may have to learn to walk afresh. The reality of God's love and the pledge of it in baptism cannot be destroyed, but we are learning to walk still. Lapses, frequent and often into the same sins, are now to be part of our struggling to our feet and we must look ahead to being able to walk, and be ready for the effort that recovery will entail.

And the image of the snake gives us fresh impetus in the Christian life, for if we can feel inside ourselves the snake still writhing, we can be humbled to accept that the fact that that writhing may be discernible in other people does not mean that they are less Christian, less brought to life than we are. In this way, the easy judgements, about those who love their homes or deny a common humanity, for example, or are oblivious of the reaching out of God or are petty-minded or vindictive – all the people like ourselves who were being written off a few pages back – are set aside. In us and in them (whoever might be covered by the word 'them') Jesus' work is taking effect, and in us and in them that work is to root out the snake and still it. And in us and in them, the effort is not to be directed at overcoming the snake but at following Jesus.

Ignore the snake, love the Charmer

Charm and *smarm* sound very much alike! We may not much care for the idea of being charmed, but let us think for a moment about that word *charm*.

We may not like the idea of being seduced or put under a spell, but that is what has happened to us. We are under the influence of all kinds of spells. Yet if we keep to the idea of seduction, we can see something important and hopeful. There is nothing seductive about one who is repellent. Seduction depends upon the seducer's ability to strike a chord in the object of his or her efforts. It may be for evil, calling out something dark or dangerous. But to be seduced by good, to be charmed by it, there must be something in us to see in the good something with which we have a natural affinity.

If we are seduced by Jesus, then it is the good in us which is reaching out to and responding to the greater, primal good in Him. We can actually experience this at work if we read or sing some of the hymns that speak of scenes in Jesus' Life, especially the Passiontide hymns. We are moved by the Jesus Who suffers and represents suffering people, the Jesus Who is vulnerable and Whom we want to help but cannot, the Jesus Who is on the cross when we have identified ourselves with the crowd.

It is incidentally worth noting that there is in us a desire for justice which we often associate with punishment, and punishment delivered in some form of suffering, and yet a desire to be spared punishment. "I ought to suffer for that" is balanced by "I don't want to suffer." The appeal of those theories of the atonement, explanations of how we are brought back to God, which are based on punishment and the idea that Jesus stands in for us have as much to do with emotion as many of the views dismissed as 'subjective' which speak of the saving work of the Crucifixion as achieved by the way it moves the onlooker. Perhaps the emotional significance of the penal substitution theories is not so readily recognized because the emotions touched on can seem more sinister. However, only in the healing or integrating of our more sinister emotions and drives can true healing, salvation, restoration be achieved.

But is seduction a good image of what Jesus is doing? Does it not imply the resignation on the part of the disciple of part of her/his humanity? The whole thrust of Christian teaching is that God wants people who can love Him, and that loving is impossible if it is acquired by destroying the very freedom that makes it true love and not the fawning of a dog accepting the occasional, unaccountable slaps from the hand of the master who equally unaccountably feeds it. Of course, any image can be pressed too far, but the basic positive fact that Jesus works to draw out what is truly human (good) in us stands.

At the risk of confusing things by piling image on image, we might use one more picture in the area of seduction that can be found in the work of some kinds of therapy. These therapies work on the basis of trust and of being guided by the therapist through what might be unacknowledged parts of one's life or experiences. At times, a piece of behaviour, a fear or a relationship problem may be incomprehensible. The therapist's task is to lead the person through his or her life to find where the explanation is located.

It is because of images like this that it has constantly been stressed that self-examination carried out as a solitary exercise, away from God, is of limited use and of great potential danger. The Creator knows His creatures well and can lead them. The therapist (God the healer) can draw on the experiences of Jesus – God inside a human life – and the Spirit can give power and rest, going at the patient's pace.

Often the picture of the therapist or psychoanalyst, especially in comedy films, is of a bearded, mysterious father-figure who hypnotizes his patients and brings them round with the words: "When you wake up, you will remember nothing." The good to which we seek to respond is the good impressed on us by the creative commandments of God, given for our growth and well-being. To be truly human means accepting our humanity as made by and for God, without the need to defend or attack. It means seeing in ourselves the image of God and our lives as best guided by worshipping Him. Sin and sins are delusions, seductions which abuse the power and knowledge in us and then pervert the image of God. A verse from the Bible which sums up all these notes is one which has provoked comment because it is not known whether the psalmist is speaking of a true likeness (which can only be found in personal communion) or a likeness which stimulates the desire for what it represents (in this case God – I shall be satisfied by having my longing re-kindled) or gazing on myself and my neighbour as we truly are, when all fear and competition and selfishness are gone. I wonder whether we are really meant to decide between these and other possible interpretations or whether we might not just dwell on the words and let them speak to us again and again. However, if sin is darkness and a night of dreams in which we chase the unreal and the profoundly unsatisfying, the following words must say something:

> And I – in righteousness I shall see Your face;
> when I awake, I shall be satisfied with seeing
> Your likeness. (Psalm 17:15)

Before you go

Which episode in Jesus' Life (apart from the Crucifixion and Resurrection) would you say sums up His mission?

From which of the stories Jesus told or the other words He is recorded as saying do you draw most comfort?

What episode in the story of the Passion most moves you?

There are many characters in the gospels who seem to have "walk-on" parts – soldiers, scribes, children, would-be disciples, officials and the like. Imagine yourself in the position of some of these and ask what impression of Jesus you would have had from that encounter. Was it cheering or painful? Did you feel distanced from Jesus or drawn to Him? Why did you feel that way?

What does it mean to you to say that Jesus lived, died and rose for you?

Which episode in Jesus' Life causes you the most unease?
Which of His stories or words causes you the most unease?
Imagine He has prefaced this account with the words, "This is for your own good."
Do not feel "got at" or nagged, but remember Jesus as sharing the pain you feel and reaching for you in your pain.

What do you most fear? Offer God that fear.
What do you most hope for? Offer God that hope.

Some work from the Bible

Jesus has been described in these notes as an amphibian and as a seducer.

Read John 4:1–44 with these descriptions in mind. (*Charm* comes from the Latin word *carmen*, meaning *song*, but the song could be an oracular utterance meant to provoke the hearer to think and act.)

In the Bible, Jesus intercedes for his disciples. We are called to be a priestly people and intercede for others. How far do we see our prayer life as bringing out our situation as amphibians?

God saw all that He had made, and it was good. God made you, and He doesn't make mistakes.

Endnotes

CHAPTER 1

1. These words are found in the third exhortation in the Order of Holy Communion.

2. David Hume, in his *Treatise of Human Nature* II.3.3 There are various editions of this work so it is not possible to give a page number.

3. "On those who think that they are made righteous by works: Two hundred and twenty-six texts", also known as "No righteousness by works.", section 151; from *The Philokalia*, Vol. 1, page 138, translated and edited by G.E.H. Palmer, Philip Sherrard and Kallistos Ware, Faber and Faber, London and Boston, 1979

4. These quotations are from a variety of sources but they are here taken from pp. 69–72 of *The Spiritual Maxims of St. Francis De Sales*, edited and with an introduction by C.F. Kelley.

CHAPTER 3

1. *Markings* Dag Hammarskjöld, translated by Leif Sjöberg and W.H. Auden, Faber and Faber, London, 1964. These words are from Auden's Foreword, p. 11.

CHAPTER 4

1. Saint Mark the Ascetic "Letter to Nicholas the Solitary" in *The Philokalia*, Vol. I, translated and edited by G.E.H. Palmer, Philip Sherrard and Kallistos Ware, Faber and Faber, London and Boston, 1979, p. 158f.

2. Saint Isaiah the Solitary 'On Guarding the Intellect: Twenty-Seven Texts', *The Philokalia*, Vol. I, p. 22

3. Quoted from *Creed or Chaos* in *A Matter of Eternity Selections from the Writings of Dorothy L. Sayers,* edited by Rosamund Kent Sprague, A. R. Mowbray and Co., London and Oxford, 1973, pp.104f. There is some consolation to be found in the saying of G.K. Chesterston that if a thing's worth doing, it's worth doing badly. The act is important and it is in the disposition to the act that virtue lies. The consequences are not always within the power of the agent to determine, nor the extent to which they measure up to the ideals even of the agent. *Well done* should thus be modified!

4. *A Matter of Eternity*, p.63

5. John Cassian, X. 10 in the edition of the Nicene and Post-Nicene Fathers, T. and T. Clarke and Eerdmans, Second Series, Vol. XI, pp. 40ff. Quite possibly, it was thanks to this material that this verse found its way into the offices, the daily round of services of the monasteries, and thence into the offices said by many clergy.

CHAPTER 5

1. The ending of that play must be one of the most nerve-shredding pieces of drama ever staged. The play should be required reading for all preparing for authorized ministry in any Christian church.

2. Lines from the *Atsumori*, translated by Arthur Waley in his *Nō Plays of Japan*, Knopf, New York, 1922.

CHAPTER 6

1. Saint Isaac of Syria (seventh century), in *Heart of Compassion*, edited by A.M. Allchin, Darton, Longman and Todd, London, 1989, p. 37.

CHAPTER 7

1. *The Philokalia* Vol. I, pp. 125 and 129.
2. From the selection from the works of Gregory of Nyssa in Henry Bettenson, *The Later Christian Fathers*, Oxford University Press, Oxford and New York, 1970, p.145. The quotation here is from the Catechetical Oration 35.

Lightning Source UK Ltd.
Milton Keynes UK
UKOW04f1625011215

263867UK00001B/30/P